Bugs, Sweat, and Fears

Bugs, Sweat, and Fears

BEGINNER'S GUIDE TO WILDERNESS CANOE CAMPING

written by
ALLAN P. BAYNE

illustrated by
BURTON PENNER

edible wild plant features by
DR. GARY PLATFORD

TURNSTONE PRESS
and WILDERNESS WANDERINGS

Turnstone Press
607 – 100 Arthur Street
Winnipeg, Manitoba
Canada R3B 1H3
www.TurnstonePress.com

Wilderness Wanderings
Box 212
St. Pierre-Jolys, Manitoba
Canada R0A 1V0
www.wilderness.mb.ca

Turnstone Press gratefully acknowledges the assistance of the Manitoba
Arts Council, the Canada Council for the Arts and the Government of
Canada through the Book Publishing Development Program.

Printed in Canada by Hignell Printing
for Turnstone Press and Wilderness Wanderings.

Canadian Cataloguing in Publication Data
Bayne, Allan P., 1945–
Bugs, sweat and fears
Include bibliographical references and index.
ISBN 0-88801-234-9
1. Canoe camping. 2. Wilderness areas—Recreational
use. I. Title.
GV790.B39 1999   797.1'22   C99-920039-9

This book is dedicated to
those who share our love of the wilderness
and to those we hope to persuade.

You will notice an anomaly throughout this book. I express travel distances, liquid measurements, and most other types of measurements in metric terms. However, canoe and paddle descriptions are expressed in imperial measurements. Canoe owners still refer to their canoes as 16-footers or 17-footers. It is unusual to hear someone call his/her canoe a 4.85-metre or a 5.15-metre craft. Paddle lengths and widths and canoe weights are also commonly referred to by paddlers in non-metric terms. Portage distances are expressed in paces, which are neither imperial nor metric; they refer to the length of a person's step. Roughly estimated, a pace is 30 inches or 76 centimetres. I hope you are not bothered by this inconsistency, as it is just another form of Canadian bilingualism. Welcome to the Canadian wilderness, eh!

Acknowledgements

Thanks to Patti and Paul Nelham for introducing my wife and me to wilderness canoeing, and to Glad and Hardy Penner for teaching us the basics of canoe camping.

Thanks to our many church friends who encouraged, supported, and participated with us. Thanks to all our paddling friends with whom we have shared an adventure. The stories throughout this book are yours. And a very big thank you to the many paddlers who provided me with canoe anecdotes and photos from across Canada.

Thanks to the supporters, directors, staff, and management of Intervarsity Christian Fellowship and the Wild-Wise Program at Manitoba Pioneer Camp for partnering with us in presenting the benefits of the wilderness.

Special thanks to our family, Curtis and Darcy Bayne and Andrea and Dan Skjaerlund, for enabling us to share our love of wilderness canoe camping with them.

Contents

INTRODUCTION

Invitation to the Wilderness

On our very first canoe trip in 1984 my wife coined the phrase "bugs, sweat, and fears" as her summation of what wilderness canoeing meant to her. Some friends had invited us on a marriage encounter that involved a canoe trip in the wilderness. This was at a low period in our life and in our marriage. In hindsight, we do not even know why we said yes. The fact that we really wanted a vacation, and they were paying for it, probably had a lot to do with it. The trip was in northern Saskatchewan on the Churchill River system. In reality, we probably did not paddle very far, but, to us, it was a major excursion. We had never paddled before. In fact, we had never sat in a canoe together before. I had paddled for a couple of hours once, with a friend, when I was younger.

The magazine *Outdoor Canada* featured a story on my wife and me following our first trip and described us this way: "Al...a little soft and a bit overweight; canoe experience nil. Barb...neat, trim, short; canoeing experience nil. Canoe going in circles." We had never experienced wilderness tenting or wilderness cooking. The bugs constantly harassed us. Everything seemed like a lot of work, and it was hot. We were in a continuous state of fear about upsetting the canoe (my wife does not swim), falling behind everyone else, encountering bears in the night, and confronting unknown dangers that might be lurking around the next bend. However, in spite of the "bugs, sweat, and fears," we experienced a renewal in our marriage, and we discovered that wilderness canoe camping was something we could do together. We didn't know it at the time, but not only would we become frequent visitors to the wilderness by canoe, we would also introduce dozens of others to this therapeutic form of recreation.

This book is my invitation to you, the reader, to look past the "bugs, sweat, and fears" and come join us in what is a very fulfilling form of recreation. As you follow the story of my family's wilderness journey throughout the pages of this book, imagine yourself there with us. The wilderness is still accessible in many parts of Canada. You do not need high-tech, expensive clothing and equipment, and you can start with a low level of paddle competency. My hope is that the information in this book is everything you will need to give you the confidence to discover the wilderness, and that the anecdotes will excite you and motivate you to come by canoe to visit the great outdoors—and stay awhile.

CHAPTER ONE

Wilderness Appeal

CATTAIL
(Typha angustifolia)

Cattails have very long, narrow, flat, swordlike leaves.
Cattail flowers appear in the form of a dense corncob-
shaped sausage with a spike on top that grows on the
end of a narrow round stem. In late summer these
cobs turn brown and feel like fur; thus the name
cattail. There are male pollen-bearing flowers on the
spike above and female seed-bearing flowers on the
cob. Cattails have extensive thick, creeping roots.

They are often mistakenly called bulrushes because
the two plants share the same habitat. Bulrushes are
leafless round-stemmed plants and they do not have
a coblike flower. Confusion between the two does not
cause a serious problem, as both have edible shoots,
roots, and pollen.

Cattails are commonly found in the shallow water
along lakes and streams as well as in ditches and
marshes. They usually grow in large colonies in heavy
clay soils.

They are one of the most useful wild plants, as most
of their parts are edible in season. The green-flowered
cobs can be cooked and eaten like corn on the cob.
The pollen can be gathered from the spike and mixed
with flour or porridge as a protein-rich additive.

In the spring the young stalks, prior to flowering, can be cooked and eaten like asparagus. The tender white core of the young plant can also be eaten raw if you strip off the outer layers and wash it thoroughly in filtered water to clean off any contaminants that may exist in the shallow water in which the plant grows.

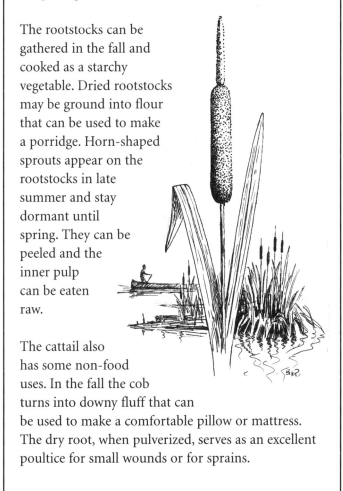

The rootstocks can be gathered in the fall and cooked as a starchy vegetable. Dried rootstocks may be ground into flour that can be used to make a porridge. Horn-shaped sprouts appear on the rootstocks in late summer and stay dormant until spring. They can be peeled and the inner pulp can be eaten raw.

The cattail also has some non-food uses. In the fall the cob turns into downy fluff that can be used to make a comfortable pillow or mattress. The dry root, when pulverized, serves as an excellent poultice for small wounds or for sprains.

The Night Before the Family Trip

It's late, it's dark, but I am completely awake. My mind cannot stop going over and over every detail on my camping lists. The food is packaged, the equipment is packed, and the canoes are loaded. My wife and I have checked and rechecked everything. Why can't I just stop thinking about those lists? I wonder how Barb can be in such a deep sleep. The 5:30 alarm will be buzzing before I get any rest. I try to concentrate on something else. I think about my son and daughter-in-law who are asleep in the next room. They have travelled 2000 kilometres from B.C. just to take part in this family adventure. I think about my daughter and son-in-law who juggled their work schedules so the six of us could be together for this trip. My mind starts to imagine scenarios involving all of us on the trail. I envision powerful waterfalls, mysterious pictographs, fascinating sunsets, and pristine beaches. I am enjoying my thoughts so much I am now even wider awake. I have to get my brain to settle down and stop spinning. I need sleep. I am so psyched up about this family canoe trip that I simply cannot unwind. It's as if I cannot wait until we put our canoes in the water and begin our journey tomorrow morning. Maybe that's the solution: mentally getting into my canoe and paddling on my journey. I picture myself climbing into my canoe. I can see the water, the shoreline of pines, balsams, and tamaracks. I hear the call of the loon and the roar of rapids in the distance. I am overcome with a

deep sense of satisfaction, and within a few paddle strokes of
my imaginary departure, I am sound asleep.

Although I go through sleepless nights before most canoe trips, that family adventure in 1995 really had me wound up! It was my big opportunity to share with my family what canoeing in the wilderness meant to me. I had canoed with my son, Curtis, a few times when he was a teenager; and when my daughter, Andrea, was 13, she and I had spent a whole month together canoeing parts of three Manitoba rivers. Although my wife, Barb, and I had not been introduced to canoeing until our very late 30s, we had taken several trips every year since. I wanted my kids and their spouses to understand what was so appealing to us about canoeing in the wilderness. It was not our goal to turn them into wilderness canoe trippers. We just wanted them to understand, from first-hand experience, where Mom and Dad were coming from because canoeing was so paramount in our lives.

It is still amazing to me, as well as to others, that I became the director of a canoeing organization at age 46. When I started canoeing at age 38 I never thought I would have any involvement beyond taking family and friends on short excursions. But trip after trip I became more competent and my interest in canoe camping increased. When I was faced with the opportunity to fill the position of director of Wild-Wise, I was more than willing to apply. Wild-Wise is a Winnipeg charitable organization that takes people of all abilities on wilderness canoe trips. With the support of my family and the help of many friends and exceptionally skilled workers, I was able to enjoy a meaningful five-year career. Although I no longer direct Wild-Wise I am still involved, assisting where and when I can, and I am still being lured to the wilderness by canoe.

Bill Mason, author, filmmaker, and canoeist extraordinaire, describes the lure of canoeing in the wilderness in his book *Song of the Paddle*. He says it was like hearing an irresistible song that beckoned him and drew him in. Once he was paddling he realized he was no longer listening to the song, but was in fact singing it.

Whenever I tried to express what canoeing in the wilderness meant to me, my explanation seemed inadequate. The words to articulate the appeal were elusive. The resulting description always sounded so subjective as to end up being inadequate. Because it is difficult to put the lure of the wilderness into words I have been on a quest to find and record all the reasons that wilderness canoe camping is so enticing. Part of what I have uncovered is that we are emotional, spiritual, and physical beings, and the wilderness experience touches all three facets of our selves. My quest for an adequate explanation may never be over but it has led me to unearth, and to spell out, some of the reasons why wilderness canoe camping is so appealing to me.

Therapy

My number one reason is that wilderness canoe camping is therapeutic. I have heard this expressed by many people in many different ways. A typical reaction is: "Something happened to me out there. I don't know what, but something good, something deep." This response may represent true feelings but it has always been a little vague to satisfy me. I want to be able to define and articulate exactly what happened.

An example of the therapeutic value is the outcome of our marriage-encounter trip which I described in the introduction. That trip marked a revival in our marriage, and the wilderness experience was the key catalyst. We have found this hard to analyze and cannot list all the specific events that brought about the change, but having to paddle together and having to cooperate with one another to deal with day-to-day chores required a heightened level of communication between us. The need to acknowledge our reliance on one another resulted in a renewed mutual respect. Sharing the excitement, the beauty, and the wonder of the wilderness precipitated a revival of our enjoyment of each other's company. Our joint belief in God facilitated a spiritual renewal as we worshipped and prayed together. We were revitalized spiritually, emotionally, and physically.

Over the years we have witnessed others who have

spoken of experiencing a renewal as a result of their wilderness encounters. A woman who has severe arthritis and is confined to a wheelchair has been on a canoe trip with Wild-Wise four years in a row. She says being able to access the wilderness brings her so much pleasure that it strengthens her inwardly, enabling her to better cope with her physical condition. One young man with a head injury was so rejuvenated that he came back changed. At the beginning of the trip he relied on his wheelchair and required constant assistance. After several days in the wilderness he stopped using his chair, and by the end of the trip he negotiated the portages on his own. When on a trip with me now, he is one of my main helpers. Another person who had suffered a head injury said that on his first trip he discovered he could still accomplish activities that he thought were no longer possible for him. He said his wilderness experience was the event that brought about a new start in his life.

Many participants say they feel a connection with something spiritual when they're in the wilderness. For most of us, being in the wilderness is a major contrast from being at home. In the wilderness there are fewer demands on our time and less competition for our thoughts, and we may experience a communion with a spiritual power that isn't able to penetrate our awareness during our hectic day-to-day lives.

I have just heard a news report about a new ailment called "adult attention deficit disorder." It results from being bombarded with a continuous overload of information every day. The report said office workers receive dozens of electronic messages daily, including phone calls, faxes, e-mail, and voice mail. It concluded with a recommendation that people suffering from this condition should involve themselves in an electronic-free recreational activity such as canoeing. It is to be hoped that anyone following this advice will leave his/her radios, Walkmans, and laptops behind. I mention in Chapter 6 that a cellphone could be useful in an emergency. Do not fall into the temptation of using it just to call home.

Many people cite rest as one of the benefits of wilderness canoe camping. In 14 years of tripping I have yet to come home rested. After my family trip my daughter-in-law, Darcy, said she would need a week of sleep to recover. I understand the potential for rest on a trip but it hasn't been my experience. My spouse likes to relax, read, and snooze—but not me. I like exploring, and I want to use every available minute of daylight to interact in some way with the wilderness. We have developed a compromise that allows her to sit in the canoe reading or relaxing while I paddle. She will often build herself a little nest in the bow out of towels, her day pack, or anything else that is loose, then recline facing me. If whatever she is reading is of mutual interest she reads loudly enough for me to hear. Sometimes she pulls her hat over her face and sleeps. This is one of the ways that we both can enjoy different benefits of a wilderness experience at the same time.

Expectation

When we put a lot of planning into something, we have an expectation of its being a special occasion. In order to take a wilderness canoe trip everyone involved has to do a significant amount of planning. There are the details of arranging for time off, deciding where to go, and determining what to take. The equipment has to be organized and loaded up, the menu planned, food purchased and packed. Taking a wilderness trip is not part of anyone's usual day-to-day activity, even for those of us who do this for a living. In each of the summers of 1996 and 1997 I led 11 wilderness excursions. Each one required a significant amount of planning. Because the occasion is special we have a higher level of expectation. During the trip, we are watching for, and mentally recording, the things that result in memories. Darcy says the memories of the family trip have become as important as the trip itself.

For years I have been taking young people from our church on canoe excursions. Some of these kids are now grown up and married. At the weddings I have attended, they have usually made some reference to the lasting memory of their canoe trips. The fact that they remember their trip and mention it as part of their growing-up experience means it was a significant event.

Adventure

The anticipation, the fun, and the excitement of continuous action alert our senses, and as a result we are inspired by what is around us. Our senses operate at their peak. We become more attuned to our surroundings. We are not in our usual, comfortable, predictable environment, and that causes us to pay close attention to everything. We hear a movement in the bush and wonder, "Is it something to go and see, or is it something to move away from?" When there are ripples in the water, is it a fish, a turtle, a beaver? The sounds in the night—are they mice, raccoons, or bears? We become aware of sights and sounds because they are unfamiliar.

Burton Penner, the illustrator of this book, introduced me to an exciting wilderness opportunity several years ago. A pair of bald eagles had built a nest near the top of a large dead pine tree that was located near and below a cliff face. By climbing up the back of the cliff face to the top you could peer across and down into the nest. According to camera readings the distance was 38 metres. In the years when the eagles were nested there I visited that site at least once annually. I took youth groups, as well as many close friends and acquaintances, to see the eagles. We made this wilderness location one of Wild-Wise's yearly destination trips. I viewed this nest when there were eggs in it and then during

every growth stage of the various eaglets that were hatched there. I climbed the back of the cliff face in the dark, battling mosquitoes in order to be in photographic position at day-break. I have sweated in a tent blind to get pic-tures of the parents feeding their young.

More importantly, over the years I watched, with great enjoyment, dozens of people as they experienced the adven-ture of a lifetime: viewing eagles from above by peering directly into their nest.

Each trip I take is a new adventure to me. I can follow the same route several times in a year, and often do, yet I do not lose the anticipation of adventure. Some trips deliver the unusual or the unexpected. On our family trip my son-in-law, Dan, while looking for blueberries, discovered an interesting cache hidden in dense bush and rugged terrain several hundred feet behind our campsite. Turns out someone had left a twelve-pack of beer and a 40-ounce bottle of Crown Royal and had never returned for them. Judging by the condition of the cardboard packaging, the cache had been there a couple of years. As these supplies were not critical to anyone's survival, Dan took his whiskey prize home and left the potentially skunky beer. We took the beer cans out on a later trip, as part of a garbage-cleanup campaign. Our family named the location Whiskey Beach. Since then I have used this story to heighten the sense of adventure in members of other groups that I have taken to that campsite. To me it was the uniqueness and the unexpectedness of the find that added excitement, not the fact that it was liquor, as I am a non-drinker.

A more recent adventure took place on Thanksgiving Day 1996. My wife and I had started a tradition of eating our Thanksgiving supper somewhere out in the wilderness. On this particular occasion we paddled with a group of friends to an island on Lake Winnipeg. The plan was to hike the island, have supper, and go home. When we returned from the hike a storm had moved in, and it was serious enough to blow our canoes end over end down the sand beach and into the lake. After we rescued and secured all our equipment we decided that we had better make a shelter fast. Dan and I carried our canoes back into some sand dunes. We overturned one canoe and placed all our gear under it. We turned the second one over, resting one end on top of the first, making a T shape, and that's where four of us huddled. The rest of the group had put up a couple of tarps in some trees. Minutes after we got under our shelter the rain hit, followed by a major hailstorm that covered the sand all around us with what looked like a coating of pure white gravel. The storm lasted only an hour, but the wind did not die down enough to permit lake travel for another hour after that. We finally got out in the dark and never did have our turkey supper. No one seemed to mind. We all enjoyed the adventure, and after all, "there is always next year."

Fascination

Another appealing quality of the wilderness is the amazement it evokes in us. All of nature is harmonized and its harmony is easy to recognize, so we cannot help but be fascinated. Nature is intriguing. It has something to teach us. We are, in every sense of the word, explorers as we are discovering new places for ourselves, often for our very first time. Nature reflects the Creator just as the lake mirrors the shoreline. The simplest way I can describe its impact on me is an emphatic "Wow!"

We often journey into a chain of lakes referred to as the Spirit Lakes, about 30 kilometres east of Kenora, Ontario. Lake Winnange has a 60-metre cliff along the shore. We can paddle close to the cliff and look up from the lake to the top.

Then we climb the cliff from the side and look down at the lake. The view from the top is sensational! Sometimes we will take our lunch with us and linger for a while.

In the same area we also like to visit Lake Teggau, which also has a high cliff, but this rock face is covered with dozens of pictographs. It is like an ancient wall of graffiti.

Several lakes we travel in the Canadian Shield have large boulders the size of small houses along their relatively flat shores. It is interesting to observe that there is no high spot nearby from which these rocks could have fallen. They look like some giant's marbles that were left scattered about the shores of the lakes.

A natural phenomenon that we enjoyed watching was the teaming up of different species of water birds late one summer. We observed pelicans, cormorants, and gulls swimming together in great numbers. They formed what looked like a large moving raft. As they travelled across the lake the pelicans splashed the water with their beaks and wings. The cormorants dove into the water, and the gulls flapped their wings above the surface. The entourage moved in this fashion for a considerable distance toward a shoreline. When they were close to shore they stopped advancing and partook in a feeding frenzy. It appeared they were working together to herd small fish. To date we have not been able to acquire any official information on this peculiar behaviour, but we have witnessed it more than once.

On another occasion we observed multitudes of suckers

Old canoe in a field of fall foliage, Herb Lake, Manitoba.

photo by Linda Butler

struggling to get up a small set of rapids in a creek. The group we were with decided to help them by catching them in the shallow water and releasing them upstream. We are not sure if they appreciated the lift, but the group sure relished the opportunity to participate in the fishes' spawning run.

Barb and I once paddled through several schools of giant carp. Most were over one metre long and I estimated their weight to be in the range of nine to 18 kilos. We do not know whether they were feeding, mating, or sunbathing, but we encountered them in weedbeds where the water was only one-half metre at the deepest. We spent a long time observing them and we enjoyed this fascinating encounter.

At another location at a different time, on a calm evening, I noticed ripples repeatedly appearing in a bay next to our campsite. Upon investigation I discovered a large school of pickerel that were herding minnows. I followed them and paddled alongside them in my canoe for over an hour before I tired of the chase.

Interaction

Environmental interaction cannot be ignored. There is nothing artificial about the wilderness. The "bugs, sweat, and fears" force us to interact with everything and everybody around us. There is no escape. Our comfort, not to mention our survival, requires that we be in tune with the surrounding realities.

While on a very rainy trip with a group of boys several years ago I noticed, in the distance, a number of canoes approaching us. They were coming from a portage that we were heading for so I was looking forward to finding out who these people were and hearing their report on the condition of the portage. As we got closer the canoes did not respond to any of my signals to rendezvous. Their occupants seemed intent on avoiding us. I noticed that it was a large group. I had counted 12 canoes, and some of them held three people. My curiosity got the better of me so I paddled across to one of the end canoes, intercepted it, and introduced myself. The discouraged guy I talked to turned out to be one of the leaders. He said they were a Scout group from

Minneapolis, that there were 30 of them, and that they were fed up with the rain. I assured him that it would end soon, as I had been out for four rainy days and this weather could not last much longer. He replied, with no enthusiasm, that they had already been out for seven rainy days and he was convinced it would never end, and that the portage was wet, muddy, and difficult. It did in fact quit raining three days later, which was about the time his trip was to wrap up. We have had to adopt an "it's raining—so what" approach. We carry on with our journey, viewing the rain as another highlight of the wilderness experience—although I have to admit that canoe camping in 10 days of rainy weather with a large group of youth would challenge me to maintain my cheery disposition.

Solitude

In the wilderness the clutter of society is gone. Therefore, even in canoe groups, we can experience some form of solitude. The wilderness, of course, is not necessarily quiet. However, the sounds of wind, water, rain, fire, birds, and animals do not compete for our attention the way the sounds of appliances, traffic, and electronics do back home. At first we experience a form of culture shock, and we may be uneasy with the silence that surrounds us. Once we adjust we discover that solitude can reveal previously-shut-out thoughts, emotions, or memories. I have heard it said that in solitude we discover "being" is more important than "having." Frequently the wilderness is described as a peaceful place. I think solitude is synonymous with peace.

Five years ago I decided to take a four-day solo trip in pursuit of pure solitude. I told my wife where I was going and when to expect me back. She responded with little or no interest. A few days later I again reminded her that I would be departing on a solo trip and waited for some reaction. When I did not receive any, I pressed her to say something. She replied, "You won't be gone for four days. You will not last two days without people and you probably will come back the day after you leave." She apparently knew better than I that as much as I desire solitude, and as much as I want to conquer some of my fears of being alone, I have a great need to share with others. So when I came home after the four days, quite pleased with myself, she was somewhat impressed, but demanded to know who I had run into out there. "Well, as a matter of fact I did run into a group at a place I visited on the third day," I told her. "They were very friendly and even invited me for lunch." Her response was, "Well, dear, it sounds as if you got exactly the kind of 'pure solitude' you were seeking."

Challenge

Seventh and last on my list, so far, of reasons why wilderness canoe camping is so appealing is the satisfaction of the challenge that it offers. This is a "hands-on" type of activity. The canoes have to be paddled, the backpacks carried. Someone has to put up and take down tents, and someone has to cook and clean. The weather and the geography present challenges that must be met. There is no escape, and on a canoe trip everyone must participate. At the end of a trip we experience a victorious sense of having overcome the bugs, endured the sweat, and conquered our fears. We feel successful. Everyone returns from a wilderness canoe trip a winner. An acquaintance of mine describes the work involved in canoe camping as his means of achieving dominion over the wilderness. This is his way of expressing the satisfaction he gains from successfully providing for himself in the outdoors.

A small group of us once took a four-day journey that should have been done in five days. The wind was against us all the way in and all the way back. Four days of hard paddling and 12 portages—what a workout! When we got home I thought I must look like some muscular bodybuilder. When I asked Barb if she noticed anything different she took one glance and suggested I had gained weight. Well, even if my physique had not changed for the good, no one could take from me the great sense of accomplishment I was experiencing.

Over the years we have developed an attitude of indifference to the bugs, sweat, and fears as well as to inclement weather. We prefer calm, warm, bug-free, sunny days but through experience we have become competent, confident, and comfortable in the realities of the great outdoors. Not everyone starts here. We certainly did not. I think it is important to do whatever you can to ensure your first wilderness experiences are positive ones. This book is written with that goal in mind.

You may have other ideas about what attracts you to wilderness canoe camping. I do not think my list of therapy, expectation, adventure, fascination, interaction, solitude, and challenge is exhaustive. My hope is that my observations will help inspire and motivate you to pursue this wonderful form of recreation, or help you better understand its appeal if you are already a committed wilderness tripper.

Jamie Benidickson in his book *Idleness, Water, and a Canoe* says that advocates of canoeing recognize great potential for personal transformation. He cites health restoration, redirected values, character building, and personal development, as well as spiritual enlightenment and renewal, as benefits of wilderness canoe travel.

Use the teepee method when portaging your canoe

photo by Donna Kurt

Roger Turenne and Martin Carver portaging a
canoe on wheels, Bowron Lakes, B.C.

There is now a lightweight cart that attaches to
canoes so you can wheel your canoe down the
portage trail. It would not be practical for most of the
rugged, rocky, fallen-tree-covered portages we travel
across, but it is a consideration for certain areas.
When it comes to carrying a canoe you can use either
the one-person or the two-person method. I prefer
the former, as two people tend to push and pull each
other too much for my comfort, especially on rugged

portages. Because solo portaging does require some practice in picking up your canoe, I recommend that people try the teepee method. First, the canoe is turned upside down. Then one person lifts up the bow (front end), leaving the stern on the ground until the centre of the canoe is at shoulder height. Then the person who is going to carry the canoe walks under the centre thwart and the person holding the bow lowers it onto the carrier's shoulders. The carrier now becomes a "canoe head."

Unloading is done in the same fashion. If you are not experienced in unloading a canoe from your shoulders by yourself, you may damage the canoe by dropping it or setting it down too hard.

Curtis portaging a canoe during
the family trip featured in this book.

Some centre thwarts and some yokes are hard on the shoulders. To add some comfort, wrap a towel or a jacket around your shoulders. Some personal flotation devices have padded shoulders to aid with portaging.

If you find you need a rest partway down the portage trail, watch for a place where you can make use of the teepee method. The idea is to place the nose of the canoe up on a branch or up in the crotch of a tree. Once you have the nose secured you can walk out from under the canoe and rest until you are ready to continue. You will not need a second person to help you get the canoe back up because it is already in position. This is also a good method to use when you want to change carriers.

On my family trip I didn't demonstrate how to properly pick up and carry a canoe until the fifth day. Because I was chastised for not explaining earlier in the journey, I am providing this tip first.

CHAPTER TWO

Wilderness Basics

LOW-BUSH BLUEBERRY

*(Vaccinium angustifolium
and V. myrtilloides)*

There are two species of low-bush blueberry plants that are common to the Canadian Shield. They are both low-branching shrubs 30 to 60 centimetres tall, and they grow in large patches. Both produce an edible berry about eight millimetres in diameter, which can range in colour from light blue to almost black.

Blueberries grow in sandy and rocky areas that have a well-drained, acidic soil. The plants are often found in close proximity to jack-pine trees. The berries are normally ripe from mid-July to mid-August. In dry conditions the season is shorter, and in moist conditions the berries may be available into late August. The berries are prolific in areas that have experienced a forest fire the year before.

The blueberry is the most popular wild fruit in the wilderness. It is not only sought after by people but also by black bears.

The fruit can be eaten cooked, canned, or raw. It is commonly used for fruit pie, syrup, jam, jelly, and fruit preserves. The leaves and berries can be dried and used to make tea. Dehydrated berries store well.

The leaves are astringent and are reported to be a remedy for diarrhea. Tea made of the leaves is said to be beneficial in the treatment of diabetes (but not as a substitute for insulin).

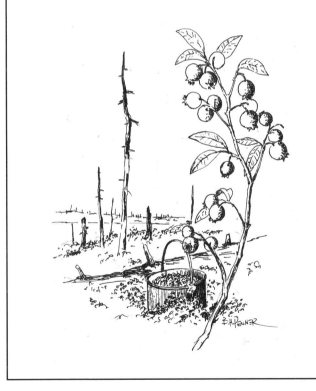

Outfitting the Family

Each of our children received a 16-foot modified Prospector fibreglass canoe with wood trim from us on their wedding days. Our son was married in 1993 and our daughter in 1994. Their canoes are almost identical. I was able to buy two similar fibreglass wrecks from a camp with which I was associated. The canoes were not usable when I bought them. I stripped them of what was left of their gunnels, decks, thwarts, and seats, and then I re-fibreglassed the hulls and painted them. I put on new oak gunnels, laminated decks, a formed yoke, and corded seats. They turned out to be good-looking canoes. The only thing wrong with them is that they weigh about 85 pounds each, which is a little heavy for portaging. I also made each of our children a paddle out of some local oak laminated with cedar. Barb woodburned into each paddle their names, a Canadian flag, and an inspirational passage. The paddles look good but they, too, are a little heavy for paddling on long canoe trips. However, because they have this nostalgic value, we included these canoes and paddles on our family trip along with my homemade fibreglass cedarstrip canoe. In place of those canoes we could have taken three 50-pound Kevlar ones, but we were willing to put up with the extra weight just to have this family experience in our special craft. Of course the photos of the trip which feature them have an added appeal for us.

The year following our marriage-encounter trip, another set of friends offered to take us on canoe trips and teach us about canoe camping. We began with a borrowed canoe, a seven-dollar garage-sale tent, and plastic garbage bags for raincoats. Neither Barb nor I knew how to swim very well, and we did not know how to read a compass or a topographical map. We were, in every sense of the word, "greenhorns." The journeys we went on seemed long at the time, but now, after years of experience, we recognize how short they really were. The first excursion we took with these friends involved a total of about 12 kilometres, and no portages, over three days. Today we would consider that an easy first day. We were a couple of very unlikelies but we were keen and eager to learn so that we could someday venture out into the wilderness on our own.

photo by Jennifer Laing

Getting ready to paddle in Algonquin Park, Ontario.

The point of this story, and of our marriage-encounter story, is that you do not need a lot of equipment or experience to enjoy wilderness canoe camping. If you are a beginner it is important to have someone along who has some knowledge and experience, and to pick a journey that is manageable for the experience you do have. We have found it helpful to agree on who the trip leader is before we begin. In times and/or places where decisions must be made, this can prevent arguments. Sometimes it is obvious who the leader is, or sometimes he/she has been pre-selected. My advice is to affirm this person's leadership and to be a good follower.

You also do not need to paddle a great distance to experience the benefits of the wilderness. We sometimes take first-timers to an island location that is within sight of where we park our vehicle. There may be some motorboat traffic and other interruptions, but it is a good introduction to the whole canoe camping experience. In 1995 we took a family of four to just such a location for a three-day trip. During the daytime we paddled as a group to nearby points of interest and did some exploring. We also walked down a portage trail without carrying any loads. All members of the family enjoyed themselves and began to catch the vision that they could actually do this, as a family, on their own.

Fortunately, for us in Canada, the wilderness is still very accessible. From where I live, 40 kilometres south of Winnipeg, I can be at a "kick-in" spot in the Canadian Shield in three hours. After two portages and 90 minutes of paddling I am out of cottage country and enjoying the solitude of the wilderness. The trip I took with my family involved a six-hour drive before we put in our canoes at a bridge along the highway. After a 20-minute paddle and a short portage we were beginning to enjoy some of the best that the wilderness has to offer.

The areas that we travel in do not require us to have a permit or any special permission. There are places in Canada where you do have to register before you go paddling, but, for the most part, the wilderness is still free. We like to check in with the Natural Resources office nearest to where we will be canoeing and let them know where we are going. We also get a forest fire update from them so we can avoid areas where fires may be burning.

Some of the skills that my wife and I took years to acquire are listed below. You may want to develop some of these before you try your first journey, although this is not necessary if you have a competent leader in your group.

Swimming

It is useful to be somewhat comfortable in the water and to have some knowledge of swimming. We wear personal flotation devices (pfd's) in all but ideal situations. In 14 years of canoeing we have never upset, but we've been with people who have. When we started, Barb not only was a non-swimmer but was very uncomfortable near the water. We decided to take swimming lessons at a pool in the winter months. She now enjoys the water more, and my swimming has improved.

One of the realities in the wilderness is that the lake or river you are paddling is also your bath location. If you are afraid of the water, or if you are uncomfortable in it, you will probably experience anxiety every time you want to bathe. The country we often paddle in has rugged, rocky shorelines that are not suitable for shallow bathing. Sometimes we need to be prepared to jump into a deep hole to cool off or get clean. You can bathe wearing a personal flotation device. In fact, it is recommended that non-swimmers test their pfd's by wearing them in the water. This is an excellent way to gain confidence in their reliability. The leader of our first canoe trip insisted that every participant be tipped out of a canoe before the journey began. (More about bathing in Chapter 7 and canoe-over-canoe rescue in Chapter 6.)

First Aid

It is wise to have at least some basic training in first aid. Having a good first-aid kit and an understanding of what is in it and how to use it is just plain common sense. Many areas of Canada offer Wilderness First Aid courses. Call your local St. John Ambulance or Red Cross office to see what they have available.

Andrea and Dan paddling in ideal conditions, close to the shore of Bending Lake, Ontario.

Paddling

Knowing how to control your canoe is helpful but not all that necessary. I have been taking beginners on canoe trips for years, and they always seem to manage to get the canoe heading in the general direction they want it to go. The advantage of learning some paddle strokes and acquiring some knowledge of the dynamics of a canoe is an increased level of efficiency. You cover less distance by going straighter and thus conserve your energy. Although this book does not include paddle-stroke instruction, some helpful techniques will be covered, such as in the Camping Tips at the end of this chapter and Chapter 3.

The Canadian Recreational Canoeing Association has member organizations in most provinces and territories. These regional chapters will provide you with information on courses and the names of certified instructors. (CRCA's address is listed at the end of Chapter 3.) Bill Mason's book entitled *Path of the Paddle*, or his video of the same name, is an excellent tool to help you learn the art of paddling. His videos are available from the National Film Board and his books are available from the CRCA, outdoor stores, and most bookstores.

Rescue

The most important thing to learn is how to do a "canoe-over-canoe rescue." There may be times when a canoe upsets too far from the shore for anyone to swim. Canoe-over-canoe enables the paddlers in the lake to get back into a dry canoe quickly and easily. Barb and I have had to perform this rescue more than once. (Details on canoe rescue in Chapter 6.)

On one occasion we were paddling with friends on a cool May-long-weekend day. We were in a channel about 250 metres from the nearest shore. We began discussing what kind of canoe they had borrowed. The husband said it was an Alumacraft. The wife disagreed, stating it was a Grumman. At that point they both leaned the same way over the gunnel to read the name that was imprinted on the side of the canoe. Their combined movement threw them off balance, and over they went. He was ready to attempt swimming to shore, but his wife's lips were turning blue and she started shivering. Because we were four kilometres from the camp we were visiting, we quickly decided to implement a canoe-over-canoe rescue to get them out of the cold water as soon as possible. Within a few minutes they were both back in their dry canoe, which, by the way, was a Grumman. The sun was shining, but the air was cold, making it most uncomfortable to be wet. As I like to carry an extra set of clothing, even on a day trip, she took my extra sweater and pants, and he took my jacket and towel.

Navigating

Knowing how to read and interpret a topographical map is very important for wilderness travel. When you've combined that knowledge with the ability to use a compass, you have become a navigator. If you are going into the wilderness, someone on your trip needs to know something about compasses and maps. There are organizations in most cities that are dedicated to teaching compass and map-reading skills, and they are often listed under "orienteering organizations." Barb and I took our training in night school from a Natural Resources officer. (More on navigating ideas in Chapter 6.)

So there you have it: swimming, first aid, paddling, rescue, and navigating. You are more than ready to start planning your first great wilderness canoe camping adventure. If you have expertise in all of these areas you will quickly be nominated leader.

Keep a small tarp handy to use as a sail

We always keep a large Canadian flag handy to use as a sail when wind conditions are right. My flag is about one metre by 1½ metres. I have placed grommets on all four corners and I have attached long thin ropes to each grommet.

When the wind is strong enough but not dangerously strong, and is coming from somewhere behind us, we get out the flag and make a sail. We begin by pulling two canoes together. If there is a third canoe we pull it in between the others so the person in the front of the middle one is sitting alongside the people in the back of the other two. The people in the front of the outer canoes tie the top corners of the flag to the tops of their paddles. They then put their paddles on the decks of their canoes, holding the paddles straight up or leaning them to the outside a little to keep the flag stretched tight. They place one hand at the middle of the flag's side and hold it to the paddle, while their other hand holds onto the canoe beside them. The ropes on the bottom corners of the flag drop to the bottom of the canoes, where the front people place a foot on them. This keeps the lower part of the flag from flapping in the wind. The person in the back of the middle canoe steers while the people in the back of the other two canoes hang onto the canoe beside them. If there are only two canoes, one of the back people needs to rudder. If there are more than three canoes it is best to separate and set up another sail.

A good wind can push you across a lake faster than you can paddle. This is a fun way to travel for everyone except, of course, the two holding the sail in the front. Everyone else just lies back and relaxes. It also looks pretty spectacular with that large red-and-white Canadian flag billowing on a lake out in the middle of nowhere.

CHAPTER THREE

Wilderness Trip Planning

FIREWEED
(Epilobium angustifolium)

Fireweed is a slender plant 18 to 30 inches tall (50 to 80 centimetres), with long, narrow leaves. The leaf colour is slightly paler on the underside than on the top. The four-petalled pink flowers appear in clusters. The seed pods are long, narrow, and cylindrical, and are filled with numerous tufted seeds.

Fireweed grows prolifically in fire-desolated areas. It can also be found in moist open spaces.

The young shoots can be prepared and eaten like asparagus. Before the plant flowers, the tender young leaves can be cooked and eaten. They are spinach-like in appearance and texture. The leaves of the more mature plant can be dried and used for tea.

Planning the Family Trip

The primary feature of my family trip was its wilderness destination, White Otter Castle, which is on a lake that is not accessible by road. This is a unique structure that was built single-handedly in the early 1900s by a bachelor named Jim McQuat. It is a three-storey log building with a four-storey log tower attached to it, giving it the appearance of a castle. The castle is built just back of a sandy beach nestled in some large pines on White Otter Lake in Northwestern Ontario. Because I wanted my family to experience the best of the wilderness that I could offer them, I took them to the greatest location I had ever been to, via the most interesting route, with the best planning I was capable of doing. I have been to this site every year, at least once, for nine years. I never tire of visiting the castle, and I love to introduce other people to the area.

My family trip was planned in the winter months, which is when I do most of my trip dreaming. We had decided to limit the vacation to family members. Extended family members were not available or were not interested. The duration of the trip was based on how long it would take, at what we hoped would be a leisurely pace, to cover the canoe route selected. The journey was manageable for the skills of the group, and it could be done in a circular fashion; that is to say, we could return on a route different from the one we would take going in and still end up where our vehicle was parked. The route included a river with negotiable rapids, some attractive waterfalls, several lakes with a variety of interesting shorelines including pristine beaches, and several not-too-difficult portages. The trip would turn out to be 72 kilometres, seven lakes, two ponds, and 12 portages over seven days.

Because the wilderness has enough potential surprises that you cannot anticipate, it is imperative that you carefully plan your trip for all the variables that are within your control. Some of the questions to ask yourself are whether you want a short or long trip, an easy or difficult trip, a well-travelled or remote route. Proper planning results in happy campers, and happy campers can turn potential nightmares into memorable experiences.

When I teach my Wilderness Leadership course I warn my students that they will find me continually reminding them to *plan, plan, plan.* The success or failure of their wilderness canoe trip will be directly related to the amount of planning they put into it. If the participants on a journey

are worried about food, comfort, safety, or the leader's competence, they will not have a good trip. People recognize solid planning and it builds confidence, resulting in participants who are relaxed enough to enjoy the wilderness.

Several years ago a friend of mine was planning a trip in the Northwest Territories. His wilderness route required that he be airlifted in and picked up at the end of his journey. There was one major error in his planning. He should have started his trip at his ending location and ended at his beginning location, as he had to paddle upstream the whole distance.

Every winter I plan more trips, or bigger trips, than I could ever possibly take. One winter I planned a canoe trip from Jasper, Alberta, to Winnipeg, Manitoba. I had calculated my distances, marked the historical sites, and even selected different towns that I would use as pickup and drop-off depots. I had planned to invite different family members and friends to paddle portions of the route with me. I forget how many thousands of kilometres the route was, but it was going to take at least six weeks of steady canoeing to complete the trip. This included paddling the full length of Lake Winnipeg, which is a very large lake that is seldom canoe-friendly. This is a trip that has been accomplished by others, but it was out of my reach. I did not have six weeks' holidays, never mind the finances to swing such a trip, nor the experience needed to navigate Lake Winnipeg. However, I enjoyed the planning process, and it helped keep me in top planning form.

Finding a Destination

Where in the wilderness should you go? Well, if you are new to canoe camping, do not start with an ambitious destination like White Otter Castle. Pick an area with rivers that are not too swift, lakes that are not too large, and portages that are well marked and not too difficult. The best source of information is other paddlers, paddle organization members, or government parks officers. I have found out about the routes I follow from other paddlers. It is important for you to realize that areas of the wilderness are subject to continuous change due to forest fires, weather, mining, logging, and man-made dams, diversions, or roads. Get current information before you even start planning.

Other than my very first trip, which was in Saskatchewan, all of my excursions have been in Manitoba and Northwestern Ontario. I plan to try other areas someday but I still have places to explore close to home.

In his book *Canoeing Manitoba Rivers*, John Buchanan lists 23 possible canoe routes in the southern half of Manitoba. This book is a great source for trip planning, as he includes level of difficulty, distance, and time required for each journey. Hap Wilson and Stephanie Aykroyd in their book *Wilderness Rivers of Manitoba* present specifics about 17 wilderness rivers and include maps, as well as detailed drawings of rapids and falls.

Hap has also written three Ontario canoe route books: *Temagami Canoe Routes, Rivers of the Upper Ottawa Valley,* and *Missinaibi*. They are all available from the Canadian Recreational Canoeing Association. Hap and Stephanie are currently working on a book that will feature the Muskoka area.

A book that I recently became aware of is *Northern Sandscapes* by Robin and Arlene Karpan. It features the sand dunes area of Lake Athabasca in northwestern Saskatchewan and provides canoe route information. After viewing the photos and reading about this area, I am determined to plan an excursion to it.

The Canadian Recreational Canoeing Association's official magazine *Kanawa* lists over 200 canoe-related titles. They include books on canoe routes in every part of Canada. The CRCA's address is listed at the end of this chapter.

Information on canoe routes can also be obtained from provincial tourism offices and from Natural Resources offices throughout Canada.

Maps

Essential to planning is a reliable canoe-route map. Topographical maps (topos) of all parts of Canada are available from the government and also are sold in some retail stores. Some of the features on topographical maps are land contours, lakes, rivers, creeks, rapids/waterfalls, swampy areas, reefs, portage trails, man-made structures, roads, trails, and clearings. On the lower left-hand corner of each of these maps is a date that tells you when the map was last revised. This is important because it lets you know how current the map information is. The topo is a very helpful tool in planning and executing a trip but you still may need to update the information on it. Something marked as a lake may now be a swamp, or a swamp may now be a lake due to changes in water levels. Portages may be relocated or overgrown.

The maps are ruled off in a grid. This aids in estimating distances, as you can quickly count the squares that cover your route and multiply their number by the distance represented by each square. I recommend the 1:50,000-scale maps because they are compact yet display the geographic details in an easy-to-read size.

Topo maps can contain mistakes. Barb and I were once crossing a five-kilometre-wide lake late in the day. It was important that our paddle direction be accurate because there were three deep bays on the other side, but only one of them had access to the portage that was our destination. We set our compass and canoed across. As we approached the opposite shore we encountered a fairly large island that wasn't on the map. We had already passed the only island that the map showed. "So where are we then?" was our big question. We knew two things for sure: we were on the right lake, and the island was real. We decided to trust our compass and continued on to the portage. Fortunately the compass was right and the map was wrong. Otherwise we would have been paddling in the dark or making camp somewhere that we hadn't intended.

Hap Wilson, the author mentioned earlier, has canoed in many parts of Canada and he confirms that maps often have errors that can cause confusion. He notes that an inaccuracy as simple as a portage shown on the wrong side of a waterfall can result in frustration or even danger for a traveller who is unaware. Maps should be depended on with caution.

I mark campsites and potential campsites on my maps with a note as to how many tents each one will accommodate. I also mark significant features such as pictographs, caves, sand beaches, old cabins, eagles' nests, beaver lodges, and anything that I come across or hear about that might be of interest. I make notes about portage trails if there is anything unusual about them, such as their condition, their beauty, or the degree of difficulty. If someone is giving me information on a particular route I mark it down right on the map. Do not leave home without a map, a compass, and at least a basic understanding of how the two work together. It is also advisable to carry a spare map in a secure location.

How Far and Fast to Travel

In planning the distance to travel it may be helpful to know canoe travel speeds. Almost any two people can paddle three kilometres per hour in no-current, low-headwind conditions. Experienced paddlers in the same conditions can cover five kilometres per hour.

It is harder to gauge portage speeds. Every portage's topography is so different, and the amount of equipment varies so much, as does the number of people. If you expect to make three trips on a portage and the portage is under 650 paces in length (1 pace = approximately 30 inches or 76 centimetres), you should allow at least an hour and a half. Keep in mind that portages are usually where the interesting scenery is found and you may want to spend time exploring or resting. You could add a half-hour for every additional 325 paces of portage. The larger the group, the more time portaging will take. I am convinced this is because more time is spent in social interaction. Everyone wants to share his/her current portage experience.

A small canoe group is four to six people; a large group is 10 or more. I recommend you keep your group at eight or under. Large groups are harder to manage in terms of helping participants and keeping track of them. People also tend to mix much better in small groups, which eliminates the potential problem of someone feeling excluded.

Stephen Sawchyn cooling off in Churchill River, Saskatchewan.

When we are on a moving trip we like to be on the water paddling by 9:30 a.m. In our area of Manitoba and Northwestern Ontario our winds tend to start around noon. The mornings are often the best time to travel. We try to arrive at our next campsite by 4:00 p.m. Somewhere in between we have lunch and a couple of breaks. We try to limit our paddling and portaging to six hours a day. A 20-kilometre day, without portages, is a big day for most recreational paddlers.

On Day 3 of our family trip we completed 15 kilometres of paddling and two portages. The first portage was 440 paces long, while the second was 880 paces. On the last portage there was a fallen tree that was lying on an angle, pointing up over the trail. It was positioned so that you could not see it if you were carrying a canoe on your head. As you approached, the tree would press against the front of the canoe and slide along the side. Because of the curve of the canoe, the tree would begin to push you off the trail as you moved forward. I managed to keep my balance, get back on the trail, and continue. When I got to the other end of the trail I put my canoe down and looked to see how Curtis was doing, as he had been following me when I set out. He was not in sight but Barb appeared, explaining that when he had been knocked off the trail he had lost his balance and ended up throwing the canoe into the bush. She said he needed a little time alone, and some space, before he would be completing the portage. His spouse, who was feeling physically exhausted, remarked that she could not believe we actually did this for fun. It was a clear signal to me that the activities and schedule I had planned were right at the edge of our ability. Curtis's frustration and Darcy's tiredness were a warning to me that if I wanted this trip to be a positive experience for them I needed to ease up on our pace. We took a long break at the end of that portage.

The question of what is more important, "the destination or the journey," needs to be considered when you are planning. I do not think one approach is necessarily more right than the other. However, if you have some participants who are interested only in the destination while others are more interested in the journey, you will have friction in your group. One of my friends, who used to help me with my youth trips, was often behind because he liked to paddle in and out of every little bay along the shore. In those days I was destination-minded and I would go as straight as I could toward the next campsite or portage to conserve time and energy. I would become impatient because we would have to wait for him. I have since become more interested in enjoying the journey and find myself wandering in and out of every bay, investigating what might be waiting to be discovered. The key is to recognize that not everyone shares the same approach to the canoe journey, and to accommodate each person's interest.

The destination-or-journey debate reminds me of the time I took a group of men to White Otter Castle. We were sitting inside the castle, which I think is spectacular, and I asked all the men to describe their thoughts about the place. The responses were typically about how, in some way, they were impressed or impacted by the castle and its builder. But the last person to speak said something to the effect of "It's a pile of rotting logs; let's go fishing." It became obvious that his agenda and mine were not parallel. I needed to give him the time and space to do what he was interested in—fishing!

Portages

"I can't believe that come January I will be fondly remembering this portage and looking forward to coming back here," Andrea stated as she set down her load during our family adventure. She, along with the rest of our group, had just completed three trips over a rugged portage in the rain. We were exhausted from the work. We were sweating under our raincoats and the bugs were aggravating us, but we all knew that what she said was true. We would remember the beauty of this location and long to be back here come winter. So, when you are planning, do not leave out portages. The good memories of the natural beauty will far outlast the bad memories of any difficulties.

Portages are subject to change because of falling trees or flooding from beaver dams. Before I have to walk them I like to get a good description from someone who has been on them recently. This kind of information can save you time and effort. Someone may advise you that the portage on the left side of the falls is blocked at the far end so you should use the one on the right. If a map shows two portages of different lengths around a set of falls or between two lakes, use the long one. My experience would lead me to presume that there is probably something wrong with the short one. To avoid longer portages I have slogged through swamps up to my waist, climbed over difficult obstacles, and tripped through tracts of deadfall. The alternates may have been longer but they were always more manageable.

Two friends of mine went on an excursion in Nopiming Park in eastern Manitoba that involved several portages. They didn't acquire updated reports on the condition of the route before departure and encountered very difficult terrain. There had been a forest fire in the area about 10 years earlier, and the resulting deadfall and thick new growth rendered the portage trails impossible to locate precisely. In order to cross from lake to lake they resorted to crawling on their hands and knees under the deadfall while sliding the canoe over the top. They reported this to be very exhausting and frustrating work. At the end of the day, with the last portage behind them, they started to set up their camp, only to discover that their tent was missing. Apparently it had fallen off somewhere on one of those challenging portages. My friends spent the night under the stars battling bugs.

Changing Campsites or Staying Put

An important point that you may not know about wilderness campsites is that they are not all that plentiful. Do not assume that you can find a suitable location to set up your camp just anywhere in the wilderness. Good campsites are hard to find. The bush can be too thick, or the ground can be too rough, not flat enough, too hard, too soft, or too low. It is easiest to find a place to put up only one tent. I have travelled for hours in new territory looking for a satisfactory location that would accommodate several tents and a kitchen area. Of course, if you go into a government park they will provide you with a simplified map and they will have rules about where you can and where you cannot camp.

You may decide to have a non-moving trip; that is, a trip where you do not change campsites each day. The big advantage to a non-moving trip is that once you put up your tent and establish your kitchen, you can leave them until you are ready to go home. Also, if you do take some portages on day trips, you will not have to carry all your gear with you. I like

Campsite on the Coulonge River, Quebec.

both kinds of trips. Quite often the people I take on excursions are first-timers and I find they get a great deal of enjoyment from just being in the wilderness and do not see a need to change locations. It is a lot less demanding physically to keep your camp in one place. I have taken people who do not even want to go on any day trips after they have set up their camp. They are content to fish, swim, and explore within 200 paces of their tent.

Canoe Choices

When I first started paddling I did not know the differences among the many designs of canoes. I used to take whatever canoe I could borrow. Now that I know something about canoes I have become more selective. I guess it is true that a little knowledge can be a dangerous thing, because 11 years ago I ended up building my own fibreglass cedarstrip canoe and spent $850 in the process. I built the type of canoe that I considered practical for my canoeing needs, which included lake and river paddling as well as transporting heavy loads. I also had some personal preferences that I built into my canoe.

The design is called a Prospector. It is 16 feet long and 34 inches wide. It has no keel and it weighs 74 pounds. It is a little on the heavy side because we wanted large decorative decks with a waterproof hatch under the front deck, and I put extra fibreglass on the bottom for added strength. I am not necessarily prescribing this kind of canoe, and I do not take it with me on all my trips. I have found the performance of my canoe satisfying, but it is a little too heavy for portaging. Fibreglass cedar canoes also require a lot of maintenance, and the rocky country we paddle in is hard on them.

You may think a canoe is a canoe, but there are many types, styles, and options. I am not going to attempt a course in canoe selection in this book. I hope to give you a few pointers on material, design, and features that may help you if you have a choice in borrowing a canoe. If you are buying a canoe, the salesperson is the one who can advise you. The first question he will probably ask you is where you intend to use it, because that will determine the type of canoe that is the best for you. The salesperson will want to know if you are planning to canoe on lakes, fast rivers, or both. He will want to know if you plan to do portage trips or non-portage trips. He will probably ask if you travel with two people or three people in a canoe. Knowing how experienced you are as a paddler will also be helpful to him.

For wilderness canoe trips, avoid buying, borrowing, or renting canoes that are over 90 pounds, under 14 feet, over 18 feet, or narrower than 32 inches, or canoes that have low sides (under eight inches of exposed side from the top of the canoe to the level of the lake). If a canoe wobbles in the floor it may be structurally weak, and when a floor bubbles up the canoe requires more paddle energy. Many canoes that are suitable for paddling around the cottage are not suitable for wilderness tripping. A wilderness-trip canoe needs to be long enough to carry your gear, wide enough to ensure stability, deep enough to be safe in waves, strong enough to deal with wilderness-trip conditions, and light enough to portage.

Aluminum canoes are basically indestructible. Occasionally a rivet will come loose if the canoe is treated too roughly on the rocks. A piece of duct tape has covered many a rivet hole for a summer season. Aluminum canoes used to be considered too heavy because most weighed 85 pounds and up, but now there are lighter-weight models that fall into the 65-pound category. Most aluminum canoes are fairly flat-bottomed, have no inward curve on the sides, but do have a keel. Because they are metal they tend to be very cold when they are in cold water or weather. They also can be hot when they are in direct sunlight on summer days. A lot of avid paddlers consider aluminum too noisy. The fact is, all canoes, because of their hollow shape, tend to be noisy if you drop anything in them or bang on the gunnels. Aluminum just happens to be a little more noisy. I suspect the traditional Canadian cedar-canvas is the quietest of all of them. I find the aluminum canoes to be sluggish, and unresponsive for manoeuvring.

There is now a seemingly even more indestructible canoe on the market, made of a plastic with a foam core called Royalex. It features something called "memory." If you happen to push in the side or bottom it pops back to its original shape. These are great canoes for running fast rivers that have a lot of potential rock encounters. They are also used by outfitters and camps for lake travel because they can withstand a lot of abuse that comes from multiple users. They usually have no keels. A minor concern about them is that they tend to be harder to manage in the wind than other canoes, as they ride high in the water. Their weight is usually 65 to 85 pounds, depending on the style and the manufacturer.

The Kevlar and Kevlar-composite canoes are perhaps the best for wilderness recreational paddling that includes lake and tame river travel. They come in a wide variety of designs and options. Best of all, they can weigh under 50 pounds. Kevlar is a very strong material that can withstand a lot of impact, but if it takes a direct hit from a rock in the rapids the fabric can be abraded. The other downside of these canoes is that they are much more expensive than the other types.

You may want to know something about keels. The keel is the bottom strip running from the front to the back of the canoe. It can be made of wood or metal, or it can be part of the moulded body. Keels are usually about an inch wide. The keel can add strength to your canoe and can help protect the bottom by taking some of the hits that might otherwise scrape or rupture the canoe's floor. Keels also influence navigation. A canoe with a keel tends to track in a straight line better, and tends to drift sideways less in a side wind. However, a canoe without a keel is slightly easier to turn and is more responsive in a current. If a keel is only half an inch deep the difference is barely noticeable. My preference is to give beginners a canoe with a keel, as it tends to travel in a straight line more easily, aiding them in their steering. Some canoes without keels have a hull designed to function as though they had one.

There are many designs of canoes, and different manufacturers have their own names for them. The name "Prospector" seems to be universally accepted to identify a particular canoe design. The following description of it should help you understand other canoe design options as well.

The Prospector is built for handling well in a variety of water conditions, for stability, and for the capacity to take a heavy load. It has a lot of rocker, which is the amount of curve from the middle to either end. This enables the canoe

photo by André van Wyk

Mike and Lori Paterson, their dog Marshall, and their homemade canoe, Upper Amherst Cove, Newfoundland.

to turn more easily because the ends, being higher, do not push a lot of water in a turn. The centre of the bottom sits the deepest in the water, and that is where a properly balanced canoe pivots when changing course.

The Prospector has a considerable amount of tumblehome, which is the inward curve of the sides of the canoe. This gives the canoe a lot of stability, as this inward curve means the canoe has to tip a long way to the side before it will take in water or upset.

The Prospector traditionally has higher-turned-up ends than most other designs. This is useful in the bow, as it reduces the likelihood that water will spill over the deck onto your lap when the canoe passes through high waves. The higher ends can be problematic in crosswinds because of their large exposed surface. If the canoe is not trimmed (see Camping Tip at the end of this chapter), steering can become difficult.

The Prospector is also a couple of inches wider than most other canoes. The extra rocker and width give it another interesting feature in waves. When the canoe is travelling in large waves it has the tendency to ride them rather than cut through them. A canoe that is narrow and flat-bottomed will tend to cut through the waves, but the potential for taking on water is greater. A narrow, flatter canoe is faster when you are going straight across a large area of water.

Some manufacturers are making a modified version of the Prospector. It has a reduced rocker and an increased tumblehome, and it is just a shade narrower. The result is a very acceptable canoe.

Again, you do not need to know all about canoe designs, materials, and options to begin enjoying the wilderness. When you decide to build your own or invest in a new one, then you will need to educate yourself.

Paddles

When my friends and I began paddling we were convinced that the wider the paddle the better. Two of my friends had 12-inch-wide paddles. We called them "breadboards" because they were useful for rolling out bannock dough. My arms tired too quickly when I used one of those so I had an eight-inch paddle. Today I use a six-inch paddle, and I am able to go faster and further more effortlessly than I ever could with my big one. It turned out that paddling proficiency increased the speed and distance I could travel more than the blade size did.

The length of the paddle should be comfortable for your paddle style. Some people say you should measure from the floor to under your armpit. The problem is that not all paddle blades are the same length, so the measurement is approximate at best. It is the length of the shaft that needs to be right. A better method is to hold the paddle with one hand on the butt end and the other on the throat, which is just above the blade. Put the paddle directly over your head with your elbows level with your shoulders. If the paddle is the right size, both your forearms should be at 90-degree angles to your upper arms. If your forearms are angling toward each other the paddle is too small. Conversely, if your forearms are angling away from each other the paddle is too big. This is not a perfect method because other factors, such as how high the sides of your canoe are, how high your canoe seat is, and whether you sit or kneel in the canoe, affect the determination of a perfect paddle size.

When I take out groups of adults a 54-inch paddle works for the average person. Tall people usually take a 57-inch, very tall people a 60-inch, and very short people a 48-inch. If you consider that you are going to raise and lower a paddle thousands of times in a day, it is advisable not to have one that is too heavy. A two-pound paddle is heavy enough. Paddles are made of many types of materials, including aluminum, fibreglass, and various kinds of wood. I used a pine paddle for eight years before it broke. I now have one made of cherry. Barb still has the first pine paddle I bought her 12 years ago. My 54-inch cherry paddle weighs 1½ pounds, and Barb's 54-inch pine paddle weighs 1⅔ pounds.

There are numerous styles of paddle blades. The more common ones are beavertail, flared-tip, and standard straight-sided. The beavertail blade is in the shape of a beaver's tail, narrow at the top and wide and rounded at the bottom. The flared-tip is a blade that is wider at the tip than at the shaft. A straight-sided paddle is one that has a uniform width from top to bottom. Personal preference develops after years of experience and familiarity with the different designs. The paddles our participants use on our trips are the standard straight-sided ones.

I use an ottertail-shaped paddle, which is narrower than a beavertail and rounded in the middle instead of at the tip. Its slenderness allows me to implement stern steering strokes with more ease. My wife now uses a beavertail, but her 12-year-old paddle has a flared tip. Both her paddles are a little wider than my ottertail and draw more water, which aids a bowperson when he/she wants to make a draw to assist in changing the canoe's direction. When we are paddling against a stiff wind or running fast water we prefer standard straight-sided or flared blades. Their width allows us to put more power into our forward motion, or to gain more control while steering in moving water, because they displace more water.

Paddles are made of many materials. The most common is wood. You can choose from aspen, pine, ash, maple, cherry, walnut, or even bird's-eye maple. Factors to consider are weight, strength, flexibility, and cost. The hardwoods are more expensive but stronger. Cherry is the most flexible of the hardwoods. Aspen and pine paddles are not necessarily lighter than the hardwoods because they are usually made a little thicker to add some strength. The least expensive are the aspen and pine. The hardwoods start at about $35. A good paddle for first-time purchasers is a wood laminate. These are very strong and very durable, and most paddle manufacturers make them. I personally do not like aluminum, plastic, or fibreglass paddles, although they are usually light in weight and very durable. The aluminum oxidizes, leaving marks on your hands, and I do not like the feel of the plastic or the fibreglass paddles.

Some people recommend that you turn the paddle upside down and use the butt for pushing against rocks or logs. This will protect the blade but can make the butt rough and cause discomfort for your hands. You can buy paddles with durable resin blade tips that protect the blades and eliminate the need to use the butts.

Tents

A tent is your primary shelter in the wilderness, and it is important that you have one that meets your needs. There are many manufacturers, many styles, and many sizes. You can have a tent that is coloured to blend in with your surroundings and not create an unnatural visual impact on the wilderness, or you can have a brightly coloured tent that will be easy for someone to spot. I am undecided about how to make that choice. Right now we at Wild-Wise use blue, grey, and tan-coloured tents.

I am not going to promote any one manufacturer, as there are many fine, quality tents, but I will tell you what I like in the style and size of a tent. First of all I like a tent that is at least 152 centimetres tall. My wife is about that tall and she likes to be able to stand up when she is changing. Not very scientific, but I am sure you will agree that this choice is politically astute. It is important to point out that the taller the tent, the more problems the wind can create. A tall tent has more surface area exposed to the wind, resulting in more pressure on the fly and walls.

I also like a tent that has a front door and a back door. I have found two doors practical. We often assign each other one of the doors so we do not have to crawl over each other if we are getting in or out, especially in the middle of the night.

Barb and I like a tent that has some room in it, so we use what the manufacturers call a four-person tent for the two of us. A four-person rating indicates enough space for four tightly fitted people and no room for gear. It is more realistic for three people.

A tent must have a fly that goes all the way to the ground to keep out driving rain. It should also have "no-see-um screens" to keep out those tiny little black flies, and it must have a heavy-duty floor that is waterproof.

I always use a groundsheet to give the floor longevity. The groundsheet should be a few centimetres smaller than the tent floor. If it is exposed anywhere around the tent, fold it under. When a groundsheet sticks out from under a tent, rain can land on it and then run between the sheet and the floor. The pressure of your body can force water through the tent floor into your sleeping bag.

The weight of a tent becomes important when you are carrying it over portages. Most of the Wild-Wise four-person tents weigh about 4½ kilos each when they and their fly, poles, and pegs are wrapped up in their groundsheet. After we place three of these bundles in an equipment pack with shelter tarps, ropes, duct tape, and other necessary equipment, the pack weighs up to 27 kilos. I find that carrying that weight is not too bad but getting it up on my back without any assistance can be strenuous. I am not the mountain-man type, although I have friends who will carry a 30-kilo pack and a 25-kilo canoe and take time to stop and talk to you along the trail.

In 1996, while on a trip with a group, I experienced a serious rainstorm at about 2:00 a.m. I remember waking to the loud noise of raging wind, pouring rain, and a shaking tent. My first concern was that a tree would blow down on one of the tents. I knew the tents could not blow away with the weight of people and gear in them. While I was listening intently for any signs of life from the other two tents I felt a fine spray of water blowing against my face. I thought I must have left the screen open, but I had not. Then I thought the wind must be blowing the rain right through the zippers, so I felt along them in the dark. Not only was the water coming from the zippers but it was also being driven right through the nylon. I had never been in a tent in such a serious storm before. I sat up in my sleeping bag to listen. At about that time I felt water pouring on my head as though I were in a shower. I started to grope around for a flashlight, only to discover there was about five centimetres of water in the bottom of the tent. Everything was soaked. The guy next to me sat up, and I asked him if he was wet. He assured me he was. Trying to make light of our situation, I asked if this was what it's like to sleep in a waterbed in the wilderness. He said, "No, rather this would be the same as a broken waterbed in the wilderness." Just then a light appeared on our tent wall and one of my helpers came to inform me that everyone's tent fly, including mine, had blown away and everyone was soaked. Without a fly even an expensive tent does not keep out the rain. We slogged around in the dark, found the flies in the bush, put them back on, advised everyone to stay put until daybreak, and lay back down on our beds of water. It was too dark and too windy and too rainy to attempt improvising an alternate shelter. That is the worst experience I ever had in a tent.

When I was telling some friends this story they were quick to advise me that I should have one of those tents with waterproof floors that go about 10 centimetres up the walls. I explained to them that those really good waterproof floors will also hold about 10 centimetres of water.

When to Go

There are lots of considerations about when you should take your wilderness journey, unless, of course, you have no choice. The best time to go is when you can get away long enough to complete your planned trip. If you are going to a high-traffic area you may want to avoid long weekends. Campsites may already be occupied and you may encounter people annoyances. There are certain seasonal conditions to consider. In our region May and September can be windy and rainy, while July can be very hot and June and August unpredictable. Rivers can be at flood levels or dangerous levels until early June, while in late August and September they can be too dry to paddle. Mountain streams and rivers can reach their high levels in July when the mountain snow and ice are rapidly melting in the summer heat. In some areas droves of fishermen fly into wilderness locations, and at certain times the wilderness is overrun with hunters. You need to learn the seasonal characteristics of the region you intend to paddle. In our area bugs are bad in June and July but do ease up in August and September.

On one of my youth adventure trips years ago I took a group of young teenagers to a popular tourist area on a long weekend. This was in a location that has no portages so a lot

Taking a break on the North Ottawa River, Ontario.

of campers who used motorboats were also heading out into the region. The campsites were government-designated, and as we journeyed we found they were all occupied. We eventually set up camp at 7:00 p.m. on a non-designated site a long way from our starting point. The youths were tired, hungry, and not looking forward to the long paddle back.

The next time I was planning to take a trip to the same place, I thought I would get smart. I sent a couple of helpers out ahead of the weekend to claim a campsite by setting up tents on the location we wanted. When we arrived there we found that the park warden had, sometime before our group arrived, posted the site as closed due to overuse. Sometimes you cannot win. I have not returned to that area since.

Each May on the long weekend we take our first Wild-Wise trip of the year. We call it our "summer warm-up." This is the trip on which I train any new staff and we get to make sure all our equipment is in good operating condition. In 1996 there was still ice on the lake we had chosen to paddle. None of us had ever paddled in ice before. We managed to go about four kilometres up a protected channel that had only some small ice floes, but the main part of the lake was covered in one large sheet of ice. One morning we went paddling to explore the edges of the large ice floes. We would find cracks and channels in the big floes that we could squeeze through with our canoes. It was quite fascinating to paddle in the ice and watch the clouds of vapour rise from them, creating a scenic mist. Some of the group wanted to attempt to reach an island, about a kilometre across the ice, that would appear and disappear through the vapour. It has a blue heron rookery on it every spring, and it is an enticing place to visit. I recommended that we wait until after lunch because if the wind came up we could be trapped on the island or, worse, be marooned out on some dangerous large ice floes. Before lunch was over a breeze did begin to blow and the ice started to move. We had to load up quickly and return to an ice-free channel or risk having our canoes crushed in the ice. From the safety of the wind-protected channel we watched floes crashing and piling up on shore-lines in the distance as the ice was pushed by the wind's pressure. For us it was another canoe experience to add to our logs, but that kind of seasonal condition is not for everyone.

Who Can Go

People of all abilities, subject to your own competence to aid them, can go canoeing. Wild-Wise, the charitable organiza-tion that I worked with for five years, has guided many peo-ple of varying abilities on wilderness canoe trips. Wild-Wise has taken people with physical disabilities and mental dis-abilities, as well as people with no disabilities. We have taken eight-month-old babies, pregnant women, 76-year-old grandfathers, paraplegics, quadriplegics, people with head injuries, people of all ages and sizes. If you have been reading some of the wilderness magazines you may have the impression that only the so-called "beautiful" people can access the wilderness. Don't be intimidated. You do not have to be a magazine model in expensive outdoor clothing to enjoy one of Canada's traditional modes of wilderness travel. Canoeing is definitely for everyone.

The Canadian Recreational Canoeing Association has produced a 30-minute video entitled *Canoeing Is for Everyone*. The association can be reached at:

P.O. Box 398,

Merrickville, Ontario, K0G 1N0;

phone: 613-269-2910; fax: 613-269-2908;

e-mail: staff@crca.ca; internet: http://www.crca.ca/

Wild-Wise can be contacted care of:

Pioneer Camps of Canada,

230 Sherbrook Street,

Winnipeg, Manitoba, R3B 2B6;

phone: 204-788-1070; fax: 204-788-1001;

e-mail: ivcf@pangea.ca

Information on my Wilderness Leadership course can be obtained by contacting:

Providence College,

Otterburne, Manitoba, R0A 1G0;

phone: 1-800-666-7768; fax: 204-433-7158;

e-mail: mlittle@providence.mb.ca

CAMPING TIP #3

Trim your canoe for ease of control

To trim a canoe means to balance your load so that the front and the back are sitting at the same height. I usually do this once I am loaded and on the water. I look at other canoes from the side and advise the occupants while they shift some of their load around. They then view my canoe and advise me. It helps if you can do a reasonable estimation when you first load your canoe. The purpose of this is for ease of paddling and steering. If your front is lower than the back, the canoe tends to require more exaggerated steering strokes from the person in the back (stern). A moderate difference is not very noticeable. The same thing happens if you have the front higher than the back, although this poses less difficulty. If I have a headwind I shift the weight so the stern is a little higher than the bow in order to make steering really easy. The wind then treats the canoe like a weather vane and keeps the canoe facing into it. If your bow is even a little bit higher, the person in the stern will be continuously fighting to maintain the canoe on a straight course because the wind is pushing against the higher end. The opposite is true for a tailwind: I adjust the load so the bow is a little lighter and the air currents keep the canoe pointing downwind. If the back is a little higher than the bow, the canoe will tend to travel forward at an angle, which also creates a steering problem. Either one of these situations can be very tiring, never mind frustrating, especially to beginners. Picturing your canoe as a weather vane should help you to make the appropriate adjustments.

We also load our canoes so that the packs and equipment do not extend above the height of the sides. The purpose is to increase the stability of the canoe. Everything that sits above the gunnels (top edge of the sides), including your upper body, is weight that can increase the canoe's potential to upset. We drop to our knees when we are in rapids, waves, or large motorboat wakes. This increases the stability even more by getting most of the body weight below the gunnel line. If you drop into a kneeling position with your back resting against the canoe seat, you will find it quite comfortable and not at all hard on your knees.

photo courtesy of Wild-Wise

My co-worker Borden Smid (in front of canoe) and I shooting a set of rapids on the Turtle River, Ontario.

CHAPTER FOUR

Wilderness Equipment

EDIBLE WILD PLANT TIP #4
— by Dr. Gary Platford

LABRADOR TEA
(Ledum groenlandicum)

Labrador Tea is a low-growing evergreen shrub. The five-petalled white flowers are arranged in showy clusters. The upper surfaces of the leathery leaves are green and the undersides are covered with rusty-coloured, wool-like hairs. The edges of the leaves are rolled. (A similar but poisonous plant called Sheep's Laurel has white hairs under the leaves.)

The three-foot-high (90-centimetre) plant grows in moist bogs in association with sphagnum moss and black spruces.

The leaves and flowers can be dried and used to make tea. The leaves can also serve as a bay leaf substitute. The tea has been used as a tonic to treat asthma and colds, and as an ointment to treat skin sores and insect bites.

CAUTION: To prevent the release of toxins, never steep leaves for longer than ten minutes, and never boil them. The tea should be consumed in moderation.

Family Preferences

My daughter Andrea and her husband Dan preferred to share a backpack for their clothing and personal items. On the fourth day of our family trip they realized that the bottom of their pack was wet and sticky. Upon investigation they discovered that the cap on their low-suds shampoo had come off. We gathered the spilled liquid and decided that, to make use of it, we would all wash our hair. Not wanting to release soapy water into the lake, we washed and rinsed one another's heads a safe distance from shore, which would allow the ground to filter the contaminants out of our water. We cleaned the pack in a similar manner.

As my son Curtis and his wife Darcy particularly like playing table games, they brought a deck of cards, a cribbage board, and a miniature version of the game Connect Four. We had ongoing one-on-one matches throughout our journey, and the current winner was continually challenged. As well, the whole family participated in group card games such as hearts and whist. Curtis, who usually won, would demonstrate his enjoyment of games by pestering the rest of us to play well into the night.

All our plates, bowls, and cutlery were stored and transported in the kitchen pack. A person's cup is required several times a day and can be hard to distinguish from someone else's, and that can result in hygienic problems. To solve this we assigned each person a different-coloured cup. Every family member was required to clean and carry his/her own designated cup for the duration of the trip.

In order to avoid the weight and bulk of several heavy cameras, the family had agreed to bring one 35-millimetre camera. We also brought two disposable plastic ones that were compact and very light. This gave the occupants of each of the three canoes quick access to a camera in the event of a photo opportunity.

A question you need to ask yourself when you are planning your trip is what unnecessary items you are willing to take. Make sure there is enough motivation to have them with you, because after a couple of portages you may be wondering about the wisdom of your choices. Weight is not the only factor to consider. Bulky items such as large pillows or oversized sleeping bags have to be packed somewhere. They do not add a lot of weight but they can result in extra packs that mean an extra trip for someone.

I hope to be able to give you a look right inside my own backpack. I will explain what I bring and why, and I will discuss some of the things I do not bring and why. My experience as a guide for Wild-Wise has been that people do not underpack; they almost always *overpack*. One time an individual brought an electric hair dryer, along with enough soaps, shampoos, and cosmetics to last anyone a year. There are no electrical outlets where we travelled, and we encourage limited use of personal-grooming chemicals for the sake of the environment.

We would recommend that participants pack for a reasonable level of comfort because we canoe for enjoyment, not to test our endurance. The wilderness can bring enough comfort challenges without us adding to them.

Wilderness Canoe Packing List
(for lake and tame river travel)

Transportation Essentials

✓ canoes
✓ paddles
✓ personal flotation devices
✓ bailer
✓ whistle
✓ painters
✓ compass, map, & map case
✓ first aid kit

Equipment Pack

✓ tent (extra pegs)
✓ ground tarp (size of tent)
✓ shelter tarps
✓ ropes (50', 25', 15', 6')
✓ bungee cords
✓ toilet paper
✓ shovel
   (small flower-garden type)
✓ hand cleaner
✓ hand wash-basin
✓ water container
   (collapsible)
✓ duct tape
✓ flashlight
✓ headlamp
✓ pepper spray (optional)
✓ lantern (optional)
✓ sail (nylon flag)
✓ whisk
✓ candle

Kitchen Accessories Pack

- ✓ grate
- ✓ reflector oven
- ✓ saw
- ✓ hatchet (optional)
- ✓ gloves (leather)
- ✓ rope (50')
- ✓ anchor bag
- ✓ folding chair (optional)

Kitchen Pack

- ✓ stove and accessories
- ✓ fuel and funnel
- ✓ matches and lighters
- ✓ fire starter
- ✓ water filter
- ✓ wash and rinse basins
- ✓ rubber gloves and j-cloths
- ✓ dish soap, bleach, and scrubbies
- ✓ mesh bags
- ✓ water bags
- ✓ table tarp (4' x 6')
- ✓ cooking pots/handles (nesting type)
- ✓ firepit pot
- ✓ coffee percolator
- ✓ frying pan
- ✓ dipper
- ✓ pizza and cake pans
- ✓ lifter and spatula
- ✓ tongs
- ✓ wooden spoon
- ✓ knife (sharp/filleting)
- ✓ can opener
- ✓ cutlery
- ✓ bowls
- ✓ plates
- ✓ cups
- ✓ tinfoil
- ✓ garbage bags

(The food pack will be looked at in the next chapter.)

Fishing Equipment

- ✓ rod and reel
- ✓ lures (small container)
- ✓ net (optional)
- ✓ licence

Personal Backpack

- ✓ sleeping bag (in waterproof bag)
- ✓ mattress (not heavy or bulky)
- ✓ pillow (compact, waterproofed)
- ✓ rainwear
- ✓ extra runners (securely waterproofed)
- ✓ warm jacket
- ✓ wind jacket
- ✓ wind pants
- ✓ swimsuit
- ✓ underwear (enough to keep you happy)
- ✓ socks
- ✓ shorts
- ✓ short-sleeved shirt
- ✓ sweater
- ✓ pants
- ✓ hat
- ✓ flashlight
- ✓ bag for laundry
- ✓ sandals
- ✓ clock (optional)
- ✓ towel
- ✓ face cloth
- ✓ book, cards, game (optional)

Toiletries Kit

- ✓ soap and shampoo
- ✓ toothbrush and paste
- ✓ deodorant
- ✓ hairbrush
- ✓ mirror
- ✓ personal medicines
- ✓ cosmetics (basics)
- ✓ razor and cream

Fanny Pack

- ✓ insect repellent
- ✓ sunblock
- ✓ sunglasses
- ✓ extra glasses
- ✓ tie for glasses
- ✓ multi-use tool
- ✓ camera (optional)
- ✓ binoculars (optional)

Transportation Essentials

The most important thing to pack is your attitude. You may be out of your comfort zone with the bugs, sweat, and fears, but if you have an attitude of tolerance you can be assured of a more enjoyable experience.

We have discussed canoe types in Chapter 3, and so will not be adding anything to those comments here. We at Wild-Wise find it best to have two people per canoe. Occasionally we have a duffer (a third, non-paddling person) riding in the middle. In most cases this is someone too young, too old, or too disabled to paddle. Two paddlers have a hard enough time getting their paddling coordinated without adding a third. If someone is going to travel solo he/she needs to be trained, as solo paddling takes more skill than tandem paddling.

In addition to having one paddle for each paddler, it is advisable to have at least one spare paddle per canoe. Paddles can break, and people must also lose them because I have found other people's paddles out in the wilderness.

More than one paddle is awkward to portage. We use a hockey-stick bag to portage our paddles. This bag holds up to 18 paddles, and one person can carry all of them in one trip.

Pfd's are personal flotation devices. There is a difference between a pfd and a life jacket. A life jacket is designed to keep you upright and your head out of the water even if you are unconscious, while a pfd just keeps your body afloat. It is important to have a pfd that fits tightly enough so it won't slip off, yet loosely enough to allow you freedom of movement. It is especially important for you to be able to move your arms freely for paddling. Check the weight recommendation on the tag to be sure it is adequate for your weight. An acquaintance of mine who upset in some rapids was pulled underwater by an undercurrent even though he was wearing a pfd. He said he was held down there too long for his liking and he was looking for a new jacket with greater flotation. Test the flotation of your own pfd by jumping into the water while you are wearing it.

Canadian law requires that recreational vessels carry one Canadian Coast Guard or Transport Canada-approved pfd or life jacket for each person on board. They must be the appropriate size for the occupants. Pfd's may now be made in a wide variety of approved colours, but life jackets still must be red, yellow, or orange.

Every canoe should have a bailer. We cut an old plastic bleach or windshield-washer container in half, glue on the lid, and tie to the handle a small rope that is in turn tied to one of the canoe thwarts. Some people do not like bailers because they are a nuisance, especially on portages. But they are very useful if you travel in the rain or are experiencing waves or rapids that are spilling into your canoe.

At least one person in every canoe should have a whistle. We use the whistle to get everyone's attention or as a signal for help. It seems as if canoes are always colliding with each other or are so far apart you cannot hear one another. Often someone is heading in a wrong direction and the only way he/she can hear you is if you give a blast on your whistle. It is helpful to agree on a whistle system; for example, one blow means stop, two blows means form a group, three blows means emergency. A good way to carry your whistle is to tie it to one of your pfd straps. It is not advisable to use a pin, as that can puncture or tear the material of your pfd.

Painters are the ropes that are tied to the front and back of a canoe. I do not know what the name means or where it comes from, but that's what they are called. My dictionary verifies that a painter is a rope tied to a boat to hold it to a dock or to tow it. In any event, painters are also useful around the campsite for other purposes that will be discussed later. The painters on my canoe are each about nine metres long and they are made of six-millimetre yellow polypropylene that is inexpensive and strong. I replace them about every fourth year.

One of the ways to protect your map is to put it in a see-through map case that has a waterproof seal. I also store my compass in the same case. You may want to consider having a spare copy of your maps as a backup and storing them in a separate place.

I have already said that having a good first-aid kit and a knowledge of what is in it and how to use it is essential. We went a step further by asking one of our doctor friends, who has been on trips with us, to recommend what else we should add to our kit. He suggested some additional bandages, ointments, and medications. We hang our brightly coloured, waterproofed kit in a highly visible spot when we make camp so that everyone can easily access it. When we are travelling we make sure it is near the top of the pack.

Equipment Pack

Our tents, together with the poles and pegs, are rolled up tightly in their groundsheets. Should they end up in the water or get rained on, they would stay dry. A tent will dry quickly if you hang it up in sunny weather, but if it is a poor drying day you are going to experience the discomfort of a wet tent. All of us prefer getting into a dry one.

I carry two plastic-fibre tarps that are three metres by four metres, which I use for shelters. We store gear under one of them, and the other is for people to sit under during rainy times. That is part of the reason we bring a wide variety of rope lengths, because you never know how close you'll be to the trees, which you'll need for tying up the tarps. I use bungee cords to secure the tarp to a tree when the trees are close by. I like using bungees because they are quick and easy. They also have some give in them, which is better for the tarps in high winds, as the cords absorb the stress. There are several ways to set up your tarps. Just be sure there is enough angle so rainwater can run off and won't pool on top, ready to dump on someone.

The toilet paper, shovel, hand cleaner, basin, and water container are all required to establish a sanitary potty site. This will be covered in greater detail in Chapter 7. Suffice to say now that you need to keep the small shovel and toilet paper handy when you are travelling. Wild-Wise's equipment pack has a front pocket that holds two rolls of paper and the shovel.

The duct tape, as everyone has heard, is the outdoorsman's solution to fixing anything and everything. We carry a large roll in the rope bag along with the bungees. Camping Tip #4 at the end of this chapter describes some of the uses we have found for it.

The flashlight I use in the tent is a small one, while I keep a regular-sized one, as well as a headlamp, with the equipment pack. The headlamp is useful when you need both of your hands to do something in the dark, such as find an item in a pack.

Pepper spray is something I have thought about packing but have not as yet. We sometimes spot bears in the distance, but in all of our years of tripping we have had only two bear visits in our campsites. The reason we do not encounter bears is related to the remoteness of the wilderness places in which we camp. We do not travel in particularly high-traffic areas where bears have become knowledgeable that people and campsites add up to food. Whenever we have spotted a bear it has always run away when it saw us or sensed our presence. The two bear visits that we have had were in high-people-use areas. We also are conscious of not doing things that could attract bears. (More about bears and safe practices in Chapter 6.)

I stopped taking a lantern years ago because we almost never used it, and no one seemed to miss it. Most people on our trips have been eager to get into their sleeping bags early in the evening due to tiredness or as a means of avoiding the mosquitoes which become very active at night.

In the Camping Tip at the end of Chapter 2, I explained the reason for a sail and the method of using it. I pack my sail somewhere near the top of a pack or in my fanny pack so it is readily accessible when sailing conditions prevail.

A compact whisk is a useful item for cleaning sand, dirt, and pine needles out of your tent.

photo by Debbie Douma

Rick Shone, Dale Douma, Ken Douma, and Dan Menheer packed and ready to paddle the Seal River, Manitoba.

All of these items are packed into one equipment back-pack. We allow one four-person tent for three people. If we are travelling with couples, we put one couple in each tent and sometimes take smaller tents to reduce the weight if the group is large.

Kitchen Accessories Pack

The size of the campfire grate that I take depends on the size of the group for whom I am cooking. I have three sizes. The first is 15 by 30 centimetres for groups of four or less. The second is 30 by 40 centimetres for groups of five to eight, and the other is 45 by 60 centimetres for larger groups. I like a grate with spaces no wider than 2½ centimetres, to prevent food from falling into the coals and ashes.

I also have two sizes of reflector ovens (see photo at the end of Chapter 5), but use only the smaller one for solo or duo trips. The bigger oven holds two 20-centimetre cake pans or three 15-centimetre pizza pans, and I take it on almost every trip, as baked food is a real treat. Leather gloves come in handy for handling the oven and the grate, which can be sooty or hot.

There is a statistic that says 90 percent of all camping accidents involve an axe or a hatchet. We do not take an axe because we have found that a small saw provides all the cutting power we need for the dead wood that we use for our campfires. We do not cut down live trees for any purpose and we do not cut large pieces of dead wood that require splitting. I do carry a very small hatchet for driving in the occasional tent peg or for cutting little snags poking out of the ground where the tent will be. I never bring the hatchet out unless I need it, and I do not tell anybody that I have one along.

When it comes to storing the food away for the night we either hang the food packs up a tree or put them in a canoe, which we then float out on the lake (more on that in Chapter 6). That is the purpose of having 15 metres of rope and an anchor bag in with the kitchen accessories.

The grate and the oven are often coated with soot so they are packed into a synthetic mesh bag of the type that is used to store potatoes or onions.

The question of whether to take some folding chairs is always debatable. Folding chairs are awkward to pack in a canoe and they represent more items that have to be carried down the portage trail. I argue that at least the cook should have a chair to sit on while he/she tends to the cooking. I am usually the cook. If you do have a chair it will never be empty. Everybody wants to sit in a chair, but no one wants to carry it. I have a friend who says he hopes he is never stupid enough to bring a chair on a trip. He also hopes he is never stupid enough not to sit in one if someone else brings it. After you've sat on rocks and logs for a few days, a chair makes your backside think it has died and gone to heaven. I prefer the beach-style chair that sits a little lower and takes up less room than other types. My son and his wife were so convinced of the value of chairs in the wilderness that the Christmas following our family trip we received two fancy foldaway camping chairs complete with individual carrying bags.

Kitchen Pack

Andrea demonstrating a water filter.

Although we depend on campfires to do some of our cooking, we use stoves to avoid getting our pots and pans sooty. I carry two single-burner stoves, with wind protectors for each. I have tried others but I prefer the ones that burn naphtha. This preference is probably based on my familiarity with them. I fill up the stoves before packing them and carry three additional one-litre containers. I have found that this is enough to last a group of 10 for five days. I carry a spare stove generator and a funnel.

I have a little waterproof pouch that holds a few lighters,

a variety of matches, a candle, and some fire starter. I also keep a lighter and some matches in a separate location as a backup. Sometimes I wrap up a small amount of dry birch-bark to use on rainy days when everything around the camp-site is too damp to catch on fire.

We carry at least one water filter and educate everyone on how to use it. In Chapter 6 I will talk more about its importance. Here I want to emphasize that we place the fil-ter in an easy-to-locate spot and recommend its use for all drinking water. On a Wild-Wise trip each person is provid-ed with a water bottle and is responsible for keeping it filled. Juice crystals for the day are provided by the cook, as well as tea, coffee, and hot chocolate at mealtimes.

Washing the dishes is what I like the least. I would sooner cook anytime. We use wash and rinse basins to do the dishes. For sanitary reasons we like the water hot enough so that rubber gloves are needed, and we put a capful of bleach in the rinse water. We think sanitation is important in the wilderness and we strive to practise it. When the dishes come out of the rinse water we place them wet into a mesh bag and hang them from a branch to drip dry. The cutlery goes into a smaller mesh bag.

Nylon water bags are the greatest items for bringing water from its source to the cooking area. The water bags pack away flat, taking up little room. You can hang them in a tree when they are full, or set them on the ground. The ones we take hold about four litres of water each. Whether you use these or not, it is handy to have a bucket for water. Even a plastic ice-cream pail works well.

For a more appetizing ambiance, we use a small tarp as a picnic cloth, on which we place the dishes and the condiments. This may not be necessary, but it's a nice touch.

We have one large aluminum pot which is our firepit pot. It is the only pot that we allow to become blackened from the fire. It is used almost exclusively for heating water, and on a rare occasion we will cook in it. We preheat water in it before we use the percolator on the stove to make coffee, as a way of conserving fuel. We also have three stainless-steel nesting pots that we cook with over the stoves, and two 25-centimetre fry pans. We have several 15-centimetre pizza pans and two 20-centimetre cake pans which are used in the reflector oven. For dippers we use one-cup and two-cup metal containers (Sierra cups), which also serve as cups or bowls.

The rest of the kitchen list is self-explanatory. We carry the cutlery and utensils in a bag, and the bowls and plates fit inside the nesting pots, which in turn fit into the firepit pot. Everything on this list fits into one pack, starting with the basins on the bottom. The stove, fuel, water filter, tinfoil, and cutlery go in the side pockets, while the garbage bags and matches fit in the front pocket. If you are just beginning to wilderness canoe camp and you are budget-conscious, you can likely pick up all the pans, dishes, and cutlery at a thrift store for under $20.

Bruce Peters shows off a lake trout
he caught during my Wilderness
Leadership course.

Fishing Equipment

I pack three lures, six spoons, and several leaders and weights
into a 10-by-15-by-2½-centimetre plastic container to
reduce weight and bulk. When several people bring tackle
boxes there is a lot of unnecessary duplication of equipment
that just has to be carried by someone. I encourage people to
minimize their tackle. A collapsible rod is most convenient
for packing and portaging.

Personal Backpack

My sleeping bag is an average-sized backpacker type, but I use compression straps to squeeze the air out and cut its size in half. I use a self-inflating type of mattress. These mattresses roll up very compactly, and although they are only 2½ centimetres thick when inflated, I find them very comfortable. Wild-Wise supplies one to every participant on our excursions, for two reasons. They want everyone to sleep comfortably, and, secondly, they want to avoid having to pack all the other large mattress-type things that people might bring along. The downside of the self-inflating mattresses is that they are expensive. The second, less-expensive option would be a thin piece of celled foam about 45 centimetres wide and 122 centimetres long that will roll up into a 13-centimetre-diameter size. Most people are not aware that you need a mattress only from your shoulders to the back of your knees. From the knees down your legs do not experience any added comfort from a mattress because there is limited body weight at that point.

Your head can rest on a small pillow. I love having a pillow and do not sleep well without one. The kind I take is the size of a small cushion but it squeezes into a sack about the size of a baseball. I wrap my wool jacket around it for a little added body. You can also wrap a few of your clothes in a ball as a substitute for a pillow. Some people take along an empty pillowcase and stuff it with their clothes. I pack my sleeping bag, mattress, and pillow in the main compartment of my personal backpack.

Rainwear should be at the top of everyone's list and underlined. You definitely want to place it somewhere near the top of your pack so you're able to get at it fast. There is nothing more frustrating than having to stop to unpack your gear while you are becoming soaked. Your rain gear should be of a quality that does not rip easily. For the most part, inexpensive plastic raincoats will not last a whole trip. I have had many raincoats fall apart on me. Barb says I am too hard on my raincoats, probably because I am still very active even when it is raining. A friend of ours made two-piece suits out of waterproof nylon for Barb and me. After four seasons Barb's looks almost new and mine is a wreck. The armpit seams are ripped, the crotch has been re-sewn twice, and I have worn out the waterproofing in spots so that the suit is no longer waterproof. In a pinch you can turn a garbage bag into a rain protector by cutting a hole in the bottom to put your head through and a hole on either side for your arms. Get fancy by attaching a garbage-bag hood with duct tape!

In addition to the sandals attached to my pack and the runners on my feet, I keep a second pair of runners securely waterproofed in my pack. On most trips I do not even take them out. They are there for those times when things get so wet and cool that I just have to put my feet into something dry.

Another point about footwear is that we wear something on our feet to protect them even when we are swimming. Every time I think I have finally arrived at a location where no modern man has ever been, I spot some broken glass in the water. Sharp rocks and waterlogged debris can also play havoc with your feet, if not in the water, then on the climb out.

I like a hat that has some absorption power so that on a hot day when you dip it in the lake and put it back on your head it keeps you cool for a while. I also like a hat with a chinstrap for paddling on windy days. I have found that a cotton hat with a medium brim works for me. Barb says I look silly in it, and she prefers I wear it only in the wilderness.

The rest of the list is self-explanatory. I take one pair of socks and one set of underwear for each day of the trip. I don't recommend jeans or other heavy cotton pants because they do not dry easily. Stick with light cottons or synthetics. Layering your clothes is the way to dress, as you can add if the day gets cooler or subtract if it gets warmer. I pack all my clothing in one waterproof sack that fits in the bottom compartment of my backpack. After I fill the bag I put my knees on it to squeeze out the air. If the bag does not fit in my pack, that is my clue that I have taken more stuff than I am going to need. Most of our trips are four or five days. For longer trips we do our laundry on a good drying day somewhere along the way. People who are new to canoe camping often bring too much stuff. Sometimes we have to encourage them to leave some of it behind. One of our little tricks is to leave a complete change of clothes in our vehicle, to put on for the trip home. A quick bath in the lake or river, and clean clothes, are a good reintroduction to civilization.

Toiletries Kit

I put my toiletries in a small ditty bag that fits into a side pocket of my pack. I like the thin belt on it because it is light, but also because I can easily hang my kit in a tree for convenience. Chapter 7 includes more information about kinds of soap and methods of washing.

Fanny Pack

I strap my fanny pack onto my pack. Most of the items in it are things I may need to get at in a hurry, such as insect repellent or sunblock. It accompanies me if we are going on a hike or on a day trip because it holds my binoculars. My fanny pack is big enough that I can stick my fishhooks in it, along with a light jacket or even a sail.

How to Pack the Canoes

Barb delights in blasting me with paddlefuls of water every so often. This has caused my otherwise sunny disposition to cloud over, and I have chastised her on the pretense that such antics slow our travel speed. She has since perfected this art and can now douse me at the most unexpected times, all the while maintaining her paddle rhythm.

The bottom of a canoe can be a wet place due to rain, waves, careless paddling, or deliberate mischief of this kind. Whatever is in your packs could soak up the water, as most packs are only water-resistant, not waterproof. You can help to waterproof your packs by lining them with plastic garbage bags. Be sure all your gear is protected, or raise the packs above the bottom of the canoe by setting them on some small sticks of wood.

There are different theories about packing canoes. Some say you shouldn't tie anything down because you cannot rescue an almost-full canoe. It is better, they say, to let the load dump into the lake and to recover what you can later, after the occupants are rescued. Another theory advocates tying the load in because you cannot afford to lose any of your gear. What is a person to do? On a training trip I saw a method that I like, as it solves the dilemma the other two approaches present. The idea is to securely tie the end of a five-metre rope to the centre thwart and then loosely thread the rope through all of the packs and/or equipment in your canoe. Once this is done you tie one end of the rope, by means of a slip-knot, to the thwart. The theory is that if the canoe goes over the packs will fall out of it but will still be secured to it. If the packs are hampering the rescue, the slip-knot can be released and the packs can be put one by one into another canoe.

Barb and I in a relaxed frame
of mind returning home from a journey.

CAMPING TIP #4
Duct tape
—don't leave home without it

Duct tape is described by the Canadian TV personality Red Green as the handyman's secret weapon, but it is also the wilderness traveller's essential repair kit. Its value cannot be overstated.

I have patched leaky canoes, repaired broken paddles, mended tears in tents, rebuilt tent poles, reinforced shelter tarps, fixed rainwear, and sealed leaky food containers with it. I have seen others repair glasses, cameras, backpacks, pfd's, sleeping bags, shoes, sandals, pants, jackets, hats, flashlights, map cases, water containers, fishing rods, portable chairs, and portable potties.

The uses for duct tape are limited only by a person's imagination, and its versatility often saves a journey from ending too quickly.

CHAPTER FIVE

Wilderness Menus

GIANT BLUE HYSSOP
(Agastache foeniculum)

Giant Blue Hyssop is a tall plant (30 to 80 centimetres) with a square stem and paired leaves. The triangular leaves are coarsely toothed and have a green top and a whitish green underside. The small blue flowers appear in several dense clusters that tower above one another. The leaves have a distinct licorice-like taste.

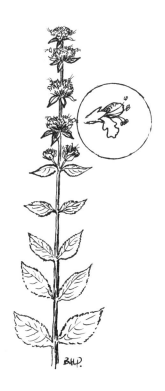

It grows in moist open woodlands and in fields along the edges of forests.

The leaves and flowers can be dried and used to make a tea that is similar to Earl Grey. Aboriginals used the tea to treat coughs and colds.

Feeding the Family

When I look through the photo album of our family trip, it is obvious that food was very important. On more than one occasion we would not be able to start eating because someone wanted a photograph of the food. We have a picture of our first supper cooking over an open fire. We also have a picture of our second supper looking nice on our plates. We have a picture of pancakes cooking, a picture of a cake baking, a picture of pizza baking, lots of pictures of all of us eating. We have pictures of lunch being prepared and a picture of fresh fish cooking in the fry pan for our last supper. In addition to these are several pictures that show us preparing food at a variety of kitchen sites. Anyone viewing the album might conclude that we had an obsession with eating. Interestingly, a lot of the photos that have been taken on all of my trips feature food and cooking. Apparently my family is not unique in its appreciation of food. Food is one of people's main concerns in the wilderness. It is right up there with safety and comfort.

One day during our trip Curtis and Dan were fishing from their canoe below a set of falls at which we had stopped for lunch. We could not hear them due to the roar of the falling water, but we noticed them holding up a great eating-sized pickerel for us to see. The blackflies were bad that day, and as I stood watching them I was shooing the flies away with my hands. When Curtis and Dan returned I asked them what had *happened to the fish they'd caught. They said I had motioned for them to throw it back in the river. I told them the only motion I'd made was to clear away the bugs. They said it looked as though I was directing them to release the fish. Regrettably, our album does not contain a photo of that fish being fried.*

Some people think you must have a plain, repetitive menu when you go wilderness canoe camping. Well, do not believe it. You could ask anyone who has ever been on one of our Wild-Wise trips, "How was the menu?" and their response would be, "Amazing." Two people stated just this year that they had not eaten that well at home. Mind you, they were both bachelors and they were both capable of stretching a story to make a point.

We do not use the commercially pre-prepared packaged food that is available in most outdoor stores. We find it more expensive than our own recipes, bulky to pack, and the portions generally too light, although the flavour is great and it is convenient. We take a minimum of canned food, as it has water in it and water is heavy. We use more canned food on non-portage trips. Also, we do not take ice or coolers. We try to eliminate all unnecessary packaging so we can conserve packing space. In our view it is important to have a varied menu as well as a nutritious and balanced one. In this chapter you will see the seven-day menu for our family trip, the shopping list, a description of how the food was packed, and a recipe for bannock. I have also included some packaging and packing tips.

One of our friends who once took a 10-day, 200-kilometre journey on the Hay River in northern Alberta used an oversimplified method of menu planning. He took a bag of flour, a bag of sugar, a bag of oatmeal, a container of oil, powdered milk, coffee, tea, spices, a can of jam, a can of peanut butter, and some nuts and raisins. He depended on catching fish and eating edible wild plants, such as berries, to supplement his diet. He said it worked out all right but there were some days when the fish would not cooperate. He is a very experienced wilderness traveller, and I would not recommend this method for beginners.

Personal Food Stashes

We have discovered that most people bring their own private stash of goodies. We discourage this practice because the presence of food in their packs can attract many kinds of unwanted critters, from ants to bears. Do you know that a mouse trying to get into your tent in the middle of the night can make enough noise that you will be convinced something a lot bigger is out there? Once a bear raided our campsite while we were gone on a day trip. In the process of try-

ing to satisfy his outdoor appetite, he practically destroyed one of our tents. We later found out that one of the people in that tent had hidden a toffee bar among his clothing. I will talk a little more about this story later on. (This is one of the bear visits referred to in Chapter 6.)

Before we depart on a trip we explain our concern about personal food stashes and ask everyone

I investigate an abandoned shack on a portage trail en route to White Otter Lake.

photo courtesy of Wild-Wise

to voluntarily surrender all goodies. We then place these goodies in with the rest of the food and grant the owner access to them whenever he/she has a snack attack. I remember one 10-year-old who was on his first canoe trip. When it came time to surrender his personal goodies he disappeared. We found him hiding behind a tree frantically devouring the cake his mother had carefully wrapped and placed in his pack. There was no way he was going to trust anyone with his secret stash.

Personal Drinking Bottles

At the beginning of a trip we provide each participant with a personal, numbered, plastic bottle full of juice that has been frozen solid. We remind people that this is the last ice-cold drink they are going to have for the duration of the trip. We also advise them that they will be responsible from here on for keeping their personal beverage bottle full. We remind them throughout the day to have a drink, as we do not want anyone to become dehydrated. Dehydration can easily happen when you are exercising and are exposed to the wind and sun. We attach a one-metre cord to the bottle so that it can be kept cool in the water (after the ice has melted, of course).

A discussion of safe drinking water comes in the next chapter.

Menu Plan for Six People on a Seven-Day Trip

	BREAKFAST	LUNCH	SUPPER	
DAY 1	At Home	On the Road	Steak Baked potatoes Tinfoil veggies Fresh fruit	SNACKS Sunflower seeds Licorice Peanuts in shell S'mores (grahams, marshmallows, caramels)
DAY 2	Bacon Scrambled eggs Toasted English muffins	Vegetable soup Crackers Condiments GORP	Smokies Instant potatoes Pork & beans Cheesecake	
DAY 3	Wild rice pancakes	Bagels Cheese Condiments Granola bars	Corned beef Green beans Couscous Pistachio pudding	BEVERAGES Coffee Tea Hot chocolate Juice crystals
DAY 4	Red River Cereal Bannock	Chicken noodle soup Crackers Condiments GORP	Pizza Chocolate cake with frosting	CONDIMENTS Butter/ Margarine Raspberry jam Strawberry jam
DAY 5	Apple-cinnamon pancakes	Beef jerky Dried fruit Cheese Granola bars	Spaghetti Pepperoni English muffins Caramel pudding	Honey Peanut butter Cheese spread Brown sugar White sugar
DAY 6	Oatmeal Bannock	Beef noodle soup Crackers Condiments GORP	Macaroni & cheese Tuna Bannock Vanilla pudding	Powdered milk Syrup Oil Sour cream Bacon bits Salt
DAY 7	Oatmeal/ Granola Raisins English muffins or Bannock	Clean up anything and everything left over	On the Road	Pepper Assorted spices Soya sauce

Shopping List for Six People on a Seven-Day Trip

Breakfast

✓ Eggs - 1 dozen

✓ Bacon - 1 pound (454 g)

✓ Wild Rice Pancake Mix - 3 cups

✓ Regular Pancake Mix - 3 cups

✓ Red River Cereal - 1½ cups

✓ Oatmeal - 1½ cups

✓ Granola - 3 cups

✓ English Muffins - 3 dozen

✓ Bannock Mix - 4 pounds (1.8 kg)

✓ Dried Apples - 1 cup

Lunches

✓ Vegetable Soup Mix - 2 packages

✓ Chicken Noodle Soup Mix
  - 2 packages

✓ Beef Noodle Soup Mix
  - 2 packages

✓ Soda Crackers - 1 box

✓ Sesame Crackers - 1 box

✓ Whole Wheat Crackers - 1 box

✓ Bagels - 1 dozen

✓ Beef Jerky- 12 strips

✓ Cheese - 1½ pounds (680 g)

✓ Dried Fruit - 1 bag mixed

✓ Granola Bars - 3 dozen

✓ GORP (good old raisins & peanuts)
  ¾ cup per person per day
  = 13½ cups

Condiments

✓ Butter/Margarine - 1½ lbs. (680 g)

✓ Raspberry Jam - 2 cups

✓ Strawberry Jam - 2 cups

✓ Honey - 2 cups

✓ Peanut Butter - 2 cups

✓ Cheese Spread - 2 cups

✓ Brown Sugar - 2 cups

✓ White Sugar - 2 cups

✓ Syrup - 2 cups

✓ Powdered Milk - 1 small bag

✓ Oil - 2 cups

✓ Soya Sauce - ¼ cup

✓ Sour Cream - 1 package instant

✓ Bacon Bits - handful

✓ Salt - shaker full

✓ Pepper - shaker full

✓ Spices - variety in small
  containers

Supper

- ✓ Steaks - 6 ribeye
- ✓ Potatoes - 6 medium
- ✓ Vegetables (carrots, parsnips, celery)
- ✓ Onion - 1 large
- ✓ Smokies - 12
- ✓ Pizza Mixes - 3 regular
-   Mushrooms - 2 cans
-   Pepperoni - 1 stick
-   Mozzarella Cheese - 2 cups, shredded
- ✓ Instant Potatoes - 3 cups
- ✓ Dehydrated Green Beans - 1 cup
- ✓ Couscous - 1 small box
- ✓ Pork & Beans - 2 cans
- ✓ Spaghetti - enough for 6
-   Pepperoni - 1 stick
-   Spaghetti sauce - 2 packages
-   Tomato paste - 1 can
- ✓ Noodles - enough for 6
-   Sauce - 3 packages
-   Tuna - 2 cans

Desserts

- ✓ Oranges/Apples - 6
- ✓ Cheesecake Mix - 1 box instant
- ✓ Pistachio Pudding - 2 boxes
- ✓ Caramel Pudding - 2 boxes
- ✓ Vanilla Pudding - 2 boxes
- ✓ Chocolate Cake Mix - 1 box
-   Icing - 1 tin

Snacks

- ✓ S'Mores - Grahams - 1 box
-   Marshmallows - 1 bag
-   Caramels - 2 cups
- ✓ Sunflower Seeds - 1 bag
- ✓ Licorice - 1 bag black & 1 bag red
- ✓ Peanuts in shell - 1 bag

Beverages

- ✓ Coffee - 2 pounds (900 g)
- ✓ Tea - 30 bags
- ✓ Hot Chocolate - 2 pounds (900 g)
- ✓ Juice Crystals - 12 packages orange
-   12 packages peach
-   12 packages iced tea

The cost of providing this food for six people on a seven-day trip in July of 1995 was just under $300. That works out to about $42 a day, $16.65 per meal, or $2.75 per person per meal.

The Menu Plan

You will notice the obvious progression in the seven-day menu from perishable to non-perishable foods. At the beginning of the trip the steaks, bacon, smokies, cheese, pepperoni, scrambled eggs, and English muffins are frozen. Prior to departure the raw eggs are mixed with cheese, green peppers, onions, and salt and pepper, and frozen in a leak-proof plastic jar. Some foods store remarkably well, such as vacuum-packed cheese and pepperoni sticks. If you protect these items by keeping the food packs in the shade, they will last up to five days. The eggs, of course, must be cooked and eaten shortly after they are thawed, to avoid health hazards.

We pre-prepare the potatoes and the vegetables for our first supper by cutting them, adding salt, pepper, and onions, and wrapping them in tinfoil ready for the firepit. The pizza is made from a standard pizza mix, with a few extras such as mushrooms and pepperoni added. There is lots of room to accommodate personal preferences when planning these kinds of meals. The cake and pancake mixes are the instant, add-water-only types that do not require any additives such as eggs. An alternative to taking icing along is to lay marsh-mallows across the cake when it is fresh out of the oven and then sprinkle a few wild berries on the marshmallow. The bannock is premixed at home and only requires water.

GORP is an acronym for "good old raisins and peanuts." The GORP is mixed and packed into individual ¾-cup bags. The mix is varied a little for different days. For example, jelly beans or Smarties may be substituted for raisins, or mixed nuts may replace peanuts. If we are taking an early-season trip or a late-season trip we will include chocolate-covered peanuts, chocolate-covered raisins, or chocolate chips, as the chocolate is less likely to melt then. During the summer months we avoid packing chocolate because anything chocolate seems to melt and make a mess even when we keep the packs out of the sun. If you do use chocolate chips in your GORP, you may find that it turns into a soft, difficult-to-eat mess. If you eat it when it has cooled down, the mixture has become a hard lump. Hot chocolate and marshmallows can take the edge off a chocolate attack.

We do not take bread because it does not pack very well and it is bulky. On some trips we have taken pita bread or pre-prepared pizza shells. We have found that English muffins and bagels pack fairly well, and they stay reasonably fresh for the whole journey. Almost all of the heavier canned goods are eaten early in the trip to reduce the weight as quickly as possible. The advantage of being the one carrying the food packs over the portage trails is that the packs get lighter every day.

You may question serving hot soup lunches on summer trips, but we have found soup to be most rewarding. For one thing, it forces you to stop and rest, as it does take time to bring water to a boil, and secondly, it is a great way to get liquids into your body.

Wendy Friesen enjoying a handful of GORP, Dibble Lake, Ontario.

Dehydration has a way of sneaking up on you, and the soup provides a palatable change from the tepid drinking water.

There are many other food choices that could be included in a menu plan, such as rice, cream of wheat, other dry cereals, or marmalade. If you are taking a longer trip, the menu can be rotated. In order to make it interesting we try to maintain as much variety as possible.

An important point to remember is that people tend to have increased appetites when they are involved in outdoor activity. Be sure you allow for unusually healthy appetites. They may be a result of the increased physical output that is experienced in the wilderness, but I suspect they are also due to some mild anxiety that I call "fear-of-shortage-of-food syndrome."

Flexible Menus

It is not necessary to stick to the menu plan. Weather conditions or travel situations may call for alterations. You can supplement your menu with fish, berries, or edible wild plants. If you find blueberries when they are in season, you can add them to hot cereals, pancakes, bannock, pudding, or cake, or you can enjoy them as a dessert on their own (see Edible Wild Plant Tip #2 on page 26). Last year we camped on an island that I named Very Berry Island because it provided us with bounties of blueberries, saskatoons, raspberries, black currants, and chokecherries. On another trip I was guiding a group of boys who were catching crawfish by flashlight in the dark, boiling them in a pot, and eating the claws and tails. With some butter, salt, and lemon pepper they actually tasted similar to lobster.

Dr. Gary Platford, who authored the Edible Wild Plant Tips for this book, has accompanied me on several canoe trips. On one occasion he was serving a cooked wild plant specimen as a supplement to our meal. An hour after supper my co-leader started scratching himself and complaining about mosquitoes. We reminded him that in fact there were no mosquitoes. "Then what are all these itchy bumps on me?" he demanded to know. It turned out he was allergic to the wild plant that Gary had prepared and he had broken out in hives. He was allergic to asparagus, and this plant, called

Andrew Daley baking supper in a reflector oven, Pekans River, Quebec.

Smartweed, was in the same plant family.

Barb and I once camped near a portage trail that was loaded with blueberries. We even had to pick the berries from the spot where we were going to pitch the tent, or risk getting it badly stained. During the course of our stay I cooked blueberry pies, blueberry turnovers, and blueberry biscuits. I baked more blueberry desserts than the two of us could hope to eat in a week. When Barb asked why I was cooking so much food I assured her we would need it. She was not convinced, since we were going home the next day. She suspected that I was hoping somebody would come down that portage trail—somebody whom I could bribe into a visit by offering fresh blueberry baking. Myself, I think it is only right to be prepared to entertain strangers.

Unfortunately, none came, and we had a lot of leftover desserts to take home. In retrospect, we should have enjoyed them in the wilderness, as that smoky flavour becomes more noticeable when you re-enter civilization. We aren't quite aware of it when we're camping, but it is definitely not as appetizing once you are out of the bush!

Packaging and Packing

Earlier I mentioned that we remove all unnecessary packaging. We also put all the components of any one meal together. For example, all the components of the supper on Day 6 would be placed into one plastic bag. The noodles would be put in the bag, along with the salt for cooking, the sauce, a bag of powdered milk, and the two cans of tuna. The purpose of this is to make mealtimes more efficient. You will not have to look for an item or try to remember what ingredients to assemble because they will already be packaged together. The condiments are packed into reusable plastic containers.

All the food is placed in stackable plastic tote baskets with snap-on lids, which in turn fit into a pack for transport in the canoes, carriage across portages, and storage at the campsite. The baskets are not waterproof but they are water-resistant. They reduce odours, are small-critter-proof, and help keep out bugs, sand, and pine needles. For our family trip we had seven baskets, three in one pack and four in another. Some people like to pack the food for each day in a separate basket but we like to divide ours into three main components: breakfast, lunch, and supper. In addition, we have one basket for condiments, another for snacks, one for hot and cold drinks, and a final one for desserts and extra items. Whichever way you organize the food, it is helpful if you can easily locate whatever meal you are looking for. At each meal we set the condiment basket on the table tarp along with the beverage basket. If you have inclement weather, the lids can remain on the baskets. The food baskets not needed for a particular meal can stay in their pack under the shelter.

My family dining on pizza, chocolate cake, and blueberry tea, on a table someone left at a wilderness campsite. Left side from front to back: Darcy, Andrea, and Dan. Right side: me and my wife Barb.

Meal Timing

On a moving trip we have a quick lunch about noon, followed by an afternoon snack around 3:00 p.m. That's the reason for the GORP and the granola bars. Often supper is not ready until 6:00 p.m. or later, and the snack helps to hold off the hunger that comes after a day of paddling and portaging. To prepare for lunch, we place the food for that meal in a day pack when we are packing in the morning. Included in the day pack are whatever cooking items we will need, plus dishes and cutlery. The condiment basket is placed at the top of one food bag, and the beverage basket at the top of the other. Everything is handy. On our family trip our lunches were never short in duration because we were too busy visiting. A usual stop should take 45 minutes, but ours were taking an hour and a half.

Cooking Methods

Methods of cooking were touched on in the last chapter in discussions about equipment. We use two one-burner naphtha stoves to cook most meals. We preheat any water needed for cooking in our firepit pot, as we do not put any other pots over the open fire. We coat the firepit pot by rubbing bar soap all over the outside so it will be easier to clean off the black buildup when we get home.

A reflector oven is a device made out of heavy aluminum or stainless steel and designed so the top, bottom, and sides fold down for ease of transport (see picture at the end of Chapter 4). Most reflector ovens are the shape of an equilateral triangle, with a shelf in the middle held up by the sides. On this shelf you place your cooking pans. A typical reflector oven, one that holds two 20-centimetre cake pans, would be 30 centimetres on each side of the triangle and 40 centimetres wide. The oven is placed so that the open side faces the fire and so the cooking shelf is level and about 20 to 25 centimetres from the open flame. The metal from the top and bottom of the oven reflects the heat onto the baking area. With a hot fire it takes about 20 minutes to bake a pizza or a cake. We use

Donna Kurt preparing a table on the Yukon River, Yukon.

photo by Irene Furgale

15-centimetre aluminum pans that are about three centimetres deep for our pizzas, and we cook one for each person in the group. When putting in and taking out the pans, it helps to have a leather glove that can act as an oven mitt.

A turned-over canoe serves as a great table. Be sure to secure the canoe so it does not move and upset everything. And remember not to set hot pots directly on the canoe.

On a trip with a youth group, Barb had baked a birthday cake for one of the girls. When she was lifting it out of the oven, the baking pan slipped out of her hands. The cake fell out and rolled on its edge down a flat rock right into the lake. The girls were in swimming and rescued it quickly, but not before it had absorbed a lot of water and had expanded to twice its size. Barb was upset with herself and the girls sensed this, so they exclaimed that the cake would be delicious in spite of its sodden state. We set the cake in the sun on a slanted rock, hoping it would drain and dry by suppertime. It dried somewhat, but the girls were miraculously "just stuffed" from supper and could not bring themselves to eat another bite. Burt Penner (the illustrator of this book) and his wife paddled by our campsite on their blueberry-picking excursion and we asked them to stop for a visit. Spotting what at least looked like a tasty cake, they readily agreed. We had decided not to tell Burt what had happened until after he had eaten his piece. When Barb asked him how he had enjoyed it, the ever-polite Burt responded that it was the moistest cake he had ever consumed. This has become our "Lake Cake" memory.

Recipes

BANNOCK

Bannock was the traditional bread of Canadian voyageurs and pioneers. Bread is important to any diet, and bannock can be ready quickly because it is made without yeast. You can fry it, bake it, or cook it over an open fire on a stick. I find the latter version too smoky for my taste. We premix our bannock so that we'll just need to add water and cook. My favourite meal when I am camping is hot Red River Cereal and hot bannock biscuits. Barb and I enjoy it so much that we make it at home often.

> 2¾ cups flour
> 2 tsp. baking powder
> ½ tsp. salt
> 3 tbsp. vegetable oil
> $^2/_3$ cup water

Mix all of the above until the mixture forms a solid ball. If it is sticky to the touch it is too wet—add more flour. If it does not mix into one big ball, it is too dry—add water. Once you have your bannock mixed, you can add berries, and also raisins if desired, or just leave it plain. From the dough, form biscuits that are 1.5 centimetres thick and seven centimetres in diameter. Slowly fry them in a pan with a little oil for 12 minutes on one side; then turn them over and cook for eight more minutes.

Fresh hot bannock, anyone? Don Maynard using a reflector oven with which we bake pizza, cake, pie, and bannock.

The procedure is the same if you are going to bake them.

To cook them on a stick, spread a small amount of the dough evenly around the end of the stick. The dough should be about one centimetre thick and should cover a length of about seven centimetres. Hold over the fire, turning frequently, for 10 to 15 minutes. When the bannock is cooked it will peel off the stick. If you use a "green" stick, it could leave an undesirable flavour in your bannock. Bannock cooked this way has been named "campfire doughboys."

BAKED FISH

There is an interesting way to cook fish without using any cooking utensils. Remove the head, fins, and entrails from the fish and add some onion and spices. Then wrap the fish in several layers of soaking-wet newspaper. Build up the fire in the firepit and, once it has burned down to coals, dig out a hole in the ashes. Lay the paper-wrapped fish in the hole and cover the fish with the hot coals and ashes from the fire. Leave it untouched for four hours. When you dig it out you will find the paper intact, the skin and scales stuck to the paper, and the fish cooked. This works for one to two kilos of fish.

Note: To minimize the impact on the environment, I recommend this method only where there is already an existing firepit. See Chapter 7 for recommendations concerning campfires.

(Baked fish recipe compliments of Jan Sjoberg, Winnipeg, Manitoba)

Use "witches' hair" to start a fire

"Witches' hair" is the name given to a lichen that grows in evergreen trees. Most often it is found in balsams. Those are the evergreens that have flat needles, and the grey, smooth bark on their trunks is covered with blisters of sap. The witches' hair is light green and is made up of clusters of stringy strands of material, five to eight centimetres long, that burn very easily.

Birchbark, of course, is the usual choice for fire starter, but it is not always available. Where birch trees are present, pieces of bark can be taken from dead trees. Stripping live trees of their bark is not advisable because this damages the trees and can kill them if too much bark is removed.

Putting some dry branches under the tarp at night, alongside your gear, is a good way to ensure a dry supply of firewood. In the absence of "witches' hair" or birchbark, the best place to find small dry sticks is on the ground under evergreen trees, near their trunks. These places are often protected from rain by the trees' branches.

CHAPTER SIX

Wilderness Safety

BEDSTRAW
(Galium sp.)

Bedstraws are low, slender plants with square stems that are very weak. The very small, narrow leaves are arranged in whorls around the stem and extend above one another. The greenish white flowers grow in clusters on stems that protrude out of the whorls of leaves at the top of the plant.

Bedstraws grow in groups in dry, open areas. They are only palatable early in the season, as they become very tough once they mature.

The young leaves and stems can be eaten raw or cooked.

There is a larger variety of Bedstraw called Cleavers and referred to as Goose Grass. It is similar to its smaller cousin, but because of its height and weak stem it supports itself by reclining on neighbouring plants.

The young leaves and stems of Cleavers can also be eaten raw or cooked. The seeds, once roasted, make a great coffee substitute.

Bedstraw and Cleavers roots are a source of natural red dye.

Family Safety

During our family trip we had to deal with the normal bugs, sweat, and fears of wilderness travel. I dislike bug repellents almost as much as I dislike the bugs, so I would not use any unless I was really being harassed. The bugs are at their worst in the shade during the day, and everywhere during the night. I would retreat to my tent when they came out in droves in the early evening. To limit my number of night trips out of the tent, I would not drink any liquids after supper. Once is enough for me. On the first night Darcy made three night trips, and each time she let a horde of mosquitoes into her tent. The second evening Curtis reminded her to reduce her fluid intake.

We travelled in some hot weather and experienced our share of sweating, especially on the portages. We reminded one another to drink lots of fluids during the day to avoid dehydration, and we took swim breaks to cool down during our travels. At the end of portages we also took breaks and, if conditions were right, we would have a quick dip. We tried to travel at a pace that was set by the slowest, not by the fastest. By the end of the trip we were all equal in our paddle speeds and daily endurance. Although we kept telling one another to take it easy and carry the lighter packs, everybody's tendency was to get it over and done with by grabbing the heaviest one. Before we shot any rapids we would park our canoes and walk over to them. We would assess them, discuss hazards, and decide upon the best route to negotiate them. None of the family appeared to be struggling with excessive fear about anything, but they were more than willing to help with the preventative measures that we took to increase our personal safety. We had two incidents during our trip. The first was when Andrea discovered a leech on her foot. She screamed so loudly that we felt certain the vibration started an avalanche somewhere. The second incident was a blowout on the trailer on our way home. Dan, a mechanic, had the tire replaced in no time at all. I now tell my friends that I never leave home without my mechanic.

Safety in the wilderness includes the trip there and the trip home. In addition to your personal safety, it also includes protecting your equipment. The way to secure your equipment while travelling in your canoe was covered in Chapter 4, but here we will take a detailed look at canoe rescue, being lost, wild animals, and some safety and health concerns.

I do not like taking any electronic voice devices with me when I am on a wilderness trip. To me they are representative of the noise clutter back home. However, I have to admit that a cellphone could be a very useful aid in an emergency. The trick is to use it only in the case of a life-threatening situation. Not all areas of the Canadian wilderness are within reach of a cellphone tower. If you decide to take a cellphone, be sure to check on the service in your area of travel.

Canoes and Safety

Another one of those interesting statistics that I have not been able to source but believe to be true is that 90 percent of all canoe accidents happen on the highway. Be sure your canoe is tied on securely. If you put it on car-top carriers, do not assume the carriers will stay put. If you put your canoe on a trailer, make sure the trailer is properly connected. I know of a high school group whose trailer-load of canoes blew off the highway two years in a row. To prevent this from happening it is important to have some weight in the bottom of a canoe trailer. The canoes are light and they have a large surface area that will catch the wind when it's blowing from the side. Do not use worn-out ropes. On a Wild-Wise trip we had a canoe fall off a trailer while we were driving down a very bumpy back road because of ropes that were too old. Fortunately, we were moving fairly slowly and we were able to patch the canoe with duct tape and did not have to abort our trip. Remember that if ropes get wet they loosen. Do a road check after a half-hour of driving to see whether everything is still tied down the way it was when you started.

Canoe and Paddler Rescue

In my experience, most canoes upset when people are getting into or out of them. Often the problem is that a portion of the keel is on something solid. The canoe then wobbles easily from side to side, throwing the person entering or exiting off balance. The canoe is more stable if it is in enough water to float. If it isn't possible to place the canoe so it can be accessed while floating, use a two-person method. The procedure for entering the canoe is as follows. Person #1 sits straddling the deck, maintaining stability with his/her arms and legs. Person #2 enters, crawling down the centre over the gear. Once seated, Person #2 stabilizes the canoe with the use of a paddle while Person #1 enters. When exiting, the method is applied in reverse.

Canoe-over-canoe rescue involves at least two canoes, the one that is swamped and one that is not. The people from the swamped canoe stay in the water beside their craft. The rescue canoe is placed so that one end of the swamped canoe is at the rescue canoe's centre. It is best if the two canoes form a T, but it is difficult to make a perfect T in some wind conditions. If there is equipment secured to the swamped canoe, the equipment is carefully released and temporarily attached to the rescue canoe.

One person in the rescue canoe steadies his own craft to keep it from tipping, while the other person in the rescue canoe turns the swamped canoe upside down. (A lot of canoes tend to sit right side up even when they are full of water.) If they are able, the people in the water can help turn the swamped canoe over. If unable to assist, they should each hang onto an end of the rescue canoe (one at the bow and one at the stern). The person turning the swamped canoe then lifts one end out of the water and places the tip on the gunnels of the rescue canoe. This is not always easy, as sometimes there is an airlock in the end of the overturned canoe

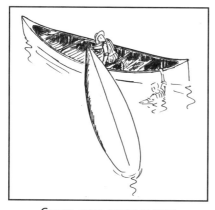

that causes a vacuum pressure when you lift on it. This can be dealt with by slightly rolling the swamped canoe on its side until the bubble breaks.

Once the tip of the swamped canoe is

Canoe-over-canoe rescue

out of the water and resting on the gunnels of the rescue canoe, the two people in the rescue canoe pull the swamped canoe completely out of the water by sliding

it across their own craft until it is centred and balancing on the rescue canoe. At this point the swamped canoe is void of water, so it is turned over and slid back until it is floating. It is placed parallel with the rescue canoe. The people in the water then come between the canoes and, one at a time, using both canoes for support, hook their ankles and their arms over the gunnels of both canoes and roll themselves into the empty canoe. The paddles and gear are then retrieved and loaded.

This description may seem complicated but the procedure is actually quite simple, and it is quick. Remember to rescue the people first and their gear last. It is very difficult for four people to travel in one canoe so the rescue needs to include the swamped canoe.

If there is no rescue canoe, rescue can be accomplished by means of an in-water recovery. After freeing any equipment, two people get under opposite ends of the upside-down canoe and throw it upward with a flipping motion. If this is done properly the canoe should land right side up with most of the water out of it. Any remaining water can be removed with the bailer. This is not an easy manoeuvre for inexperienced people and is next to impossible for non-swimmers.

Once the canoe is right side up, the people enter one at a time. There are two approaches to doing this. In the first, one person goes to each end of the canoe. While one holds it steady, the other pulls himself up and over the end while straddling the craft until he can place his seat on the deck and from there get into the canoe.

With the other method, one person gets on each side of the centre thwart. While one holds the canoe steady, the other makes a far-reaching jump to grab the thwart and then pulls himself into the canoe.

With both methods, the person who is in first then assists his/her partner and the two of them then recover the gear. I have never upset but I have practised both of these methods and find the second one the most difficult to do, no doubt as a result of my lack of agility and my girth.

If you are new to canoeing it is not advisable to travel alone. If you do travel solo, the methods above would apply. In situations where you are unable to empty your canoe, get in the canoe and paddle even though it is full of water. It will be slow going. The rule that says you should stay with your canoe if you are unable to rescue yourself is a good one. First of all, even an upset canoe offers some buoyancy, so it can help you save energy by holding you partway out of the water. Secondly, it is easier for a rescuer to spot an upset canoe than to spot a person.

One of the exceptions to the "stay with your canoe" rule is when you are in rapids. You do not want to get between a canoe full of water and a rock. The pressure of the water and the weight of the water-filled canoe would crush you. In rapids, let the canoe go! Then ride the rapids by lying back slightly in the water with your feet pointing downstream.

A paddling partner of mine tried to hang onto the painter on our empty canoe after it had upset in some rapids. The result was serious rope burns to both of his hands. We were not in the canoe when it upset, as we were attempting to "line" the canoe through the rapids to avoid portaging.

Whether you are canoeing with a group, in tandem, or solo, the safest place to paddle is close to the shore. This is also the most interesting place to paddle because you will likely spot more wildlife and see more intriguing sights along the shoreline than when you are in the middle of a lake.

In my experience, most canoe upsets have taken place within two metres of shore, usually when people are getting into or out of a canoe. Non-swimmers and poor swimmers should wear pfd's at all times. Good swimmers should wear pfd's in fast water and in windy conditions. Some strong swimmers do not like to wear them because pfd's hamper their ability to swim well. The advantage of wearing them is that they add a lot of buoyancy when you are trying to help someone else, when you are riding out rapids, or when you are trying to overturn a canoe in waves.

As I pointed out in Chapter 1, the wind can damage your canoe or even blow it away. Each night every canoe should be taken out of the water, turned over, and placed in a wind-protected location.

Personal Safety and Getting Lost

Sometimes all the planning in the world will not cover every contingency. Barb and I and another couple once met a group on a portage trail who were looking for a shortcut back to the main highway. One of their members had developed serious back spasms, and he needed to get some professional medical attention.

The portage we were on was extremely rugged, and there had been a heavy rain the day before so it was exceptionally muddy. The group's vehicle was parked several portages away on a different route from the one on which we met them. They hoped they would be able to hike out on this portage trail and then walk the 15 kilometres to their car and move the car closer to the end of this portage, as the original route back to their vehicle had too many portages on it. Their task seemed overwhelming so we offered to drive them and their incapacitated partner from this end of the portage to their vehicle. We also offered to carry him down the portage, but the only comfortable position for him was standing. He walked out with the help of his son and a walking stick. It took him over two hours to complete a 20-minute hike.

When he finally made it to our vehicle he began to feel faint. We cleared a space for him to lie down in the back of our van, and some berry-pickers we met gave him some ice to ease his back pain. We drove him and his son to their vehicle and they headed out to find medical attention.

While on our family trip Andrea selected one of the larger, bulky packs at the first portage and, with the help of her husband, got it on her back. She took about six steps up a sharp incline and fell straight backwards with the pack under her. She wasn't hurt, and as she lay there with her arms and legs flailing in the air we could not help laughing because she looked exactly like a distressed turtle. After that we encouraged her to take smaller backpacks, and although she occasionally did, she continued to tackle the big ones throughout the entire trip. It wasn't the heaviness of the pack that had caused her to lose her balance; it was the position of the load. Too much of the weight was above her shoulders. The remedy for the problem was to adjust the carrying straps so the pack sat lower on her back.

There is a story about what to do if you become lost in the wilderness. You should stop, take out a deck of playing cards, and begin to play solitaire. It won't be long until someone will come up behind you to tell you to put your black nine on the red ten or point out some other play you've just missed. At that juncture you can ask him the way out of the wilderness.

The truth in the joke is that you should stop. Stop and review what you know for sure before you go any further.

Many people carry a compass but do not have a clue about how to use one. Some people make the mistake of not believing their compasses or of using them near metal objects, which confuse the magnetic pointer. Simple knowledge such as the fact that the sun rises in the east and sets in the west can be helpful. If you know what direction you have been travelling, then you know what direction your return path needs to be.

Another simple fact to remember is that because we are north of the equator, the sun arcs in the south. We never have the sun directly overhead. It is always a bit lower than that. If you stand so that your left side is to the sun when it is positioned high in the sky, it casts your shadow on your right side. In that case you are facing west. If you stand so the highly positioned sun is on your right side your shadow is on the left, and you are facing east. In both cases north is on the side your shadow is on and south is on the side of the sun. This method gives you only very general directions and should not be used to replace a compass. It also doesn't hold true in the early morning or late evening, as the sun isn't positioned overhead in its southerly arc at those times.

As I am writing this chapter the news media are reporting that a hunter, who has been lost for three days, has just been found. According to the news report, after the hunter left his vehicle he walked east in search of game. Then he became uncertain about how to return to the vehicle. In his attempt to return he continued going east for a further 18 kilometres. If he had been familiar with the sun principle, he could have determined that he needed to go in the opposite direction to get back to his starting point. The sun was shining on the days he was lost.

Bears and Other Critters

Most people's biggest fear in the wilderness is of encountering large wild animals. The areas we travel in do have black bears. I have never travelled in polar bear or grizzly bear country, but I understand they are less shy and more aggressive than black bears. I am not qualified to give any advice on polar bears or grizzlies.

Problem black bears are the ones that have become accustomed to finding food at campsites. We call them "Yogis." We avoid travelling in areas with a lot of people traffic or in areas that have a lot of cottages because Yogis like to frequent these sites. When we do spot bears in the wilderness it is a real treat, but they run as soon as they get wind of us or see us. The bear's primary concern is food. It is not interested in having a fight with you. However, it will fight to defend its property because it thinks whatever food it has found in your campground is its own. Bears consider humans a food source only as a last resort when they are near starvation. Everyone knows that a mother bear is extremely protective of her young, and she becomes very aggressive when she thinks you are a threat to her cubs.

When you encounter bear cubs, keep your distance and move away from that area, no matter how cute, cuddly, and playful the cubs appear to be.

The people we take on trips are frequently anxious about bears. One year the girls in a female youth group were excessively concerned and could not stop talking about their fear of these animals. Before we set out on the lake, they prayed for safety but asked for adventure.

The campsite we chose was near a rundown, deserted cabin. The girls thought the cabin would be a more comfortable place to sleep than the tents, as there were several bed frames in it. They simply put their sleeping bags on top of the bare bedsprings. During the night I heard banging and thumping coming from the cabin. Upon investigation I discovered they were chasing around with an old broom and their boots, trying to exterminate mice. It turned out the cabin was infested with dozens of the little creatures. When I returned to my tent I explained to Barb that the girls were having a great adventure. They had forgotten all about the bears, and the noise they were making would assuredly scare any in the vicinity miles away. They had prayed about bears and been given mice! Eventually, realizing they could not catch any of the critters, they placed a pile of sunflower seeds by the cabin door. The mice turned their attention to the food and the group was able to get some sleep.

My first bear encounter in 1988 was the one I wrote about in Chapter 5. We were camped with a group of preteen boys on an island in a high-use lake. During the day we had left our campsite for several hours to go exploring. The island had no trees suitable for food storage, so we had left the food on the ground in the shade of small shrubs. On our way back to our campsite we were taking turns viewing the site from the lake through binoculars. When it was my turn I noticed what I thought was a food container along the shoreline. That concerned my co-leaders and me because we had not left anything that close to the shore.

We arrived back at our campsite just in time to scare off a bear who had eaten about one-third of our food supply. He must have run away with a broken bag of bannock in his mouth, as the boys found a trail of bannock flour. They started down the trail after the bear, but I called them back, reminding them that trying to catch the bear would be dangerous, and besides, what did they intend to do once they caught him?

On inspection we found that the bear had knocked down a tent and chewed holes in it to get at a toffee bar one of the boys had stashed in his pack. The bear had also completely destroyed our firepit and, from what we could tell, eaten the ashes. We'd had baked potatoes the night before, and the ashes must have contained drippings of butter. The bear ate uncooked spaghetti and polished off the jam, along with part of the plastic container. It also bit into sealed metal tins to get at the contents. That was a giveaway. This was no wilderness bear; this was a Yogi. This bear was familiar with camp food and was experienced at raiding campsites. It takes an experienced bear to know that sealed tins have food in them. We had camped too close to civilization.

We still had enough provisions to complete our trip, so we moved to another island that had trees big enough for safely storing the remainder of our food. Since then I have never left our food unattended when we are on day trips. If there is not a safe tree to put it in, I take it with me.

A puzzling thing about this bear encounter was a plastic container dripping with honey in the middle of the scattered food—the bear had left it untouched. Common knowledge dictates that bears prefer honey to ashes, uncooked spaghetti, bannock flour, and sealed tin cans. Why did the bear not eat the honey first? The boys were convinced this was a sign that we were being protected by a higher power.

My second bear encounter occurred in 1997 on the opposite end of the same lake. Barb and I were leading 12 people on a married-couples trip. One of the spouses had been overly worried about having a bear in our camp. I had assured her that I had not come across any bears on that lake in years. I was careful not to make any guarantees. I explained all the precautions we would take and with great confidence told her that we were almost certain not to meet up with bears.

Sometime after midnight, one of the individuals came to my tent to tell me that something was making a lot of noise in the kitchen area. Upon investigation with flashlights we found that our pots and pans had been tipped over and our personal beverage containers had been scattered around. Our first thought was that we had been invaded by raccoons—that is, until we picked up one of the containers and saw the large punctures that penetrated the plastic. We then went to the nearby beach and found large paw prints in the sand, prints that could only belong to something as large as a bear.

Then we heard the sounds of something moving through the brush about a hundred feet from our kitchen site, followed by a growling utterance. All of us instinctively pointed our flashlights in the direction of the noises. What a sight! Two large glowing eyes and the shadowy outline of a bear.

We yelled and banged pots and pans, and the bear withdrew further into the bush. But a short time later we could hear it growling and moving back in our direction. One of our fearless participants ran through the bush towards it, waving his flashlight and yelling as he went. This time the bear made a permanent retreat. This bear was still afraid of people; it was not a Yogi.

To assure ourselves of the bear's withdrawal, we relit the campfire and several of us stayed up to monitor the situation. When the bear did not return after a 45-minute wait we decided to take turns in pairs at keeping vigil for the rest of the night.

A bear in your camp is a big problem, but do not overlook the little critters that can also make your life miserable.

It has never happened to me, but I have heard of skunks getting into people's tents. Keep food out of your tent and keep the tent zipped shut at all times. Small rodents of every description are a nuisance and can chew holes in your tents or packs. Those cute little chipmunks and red squirrels will not respect your equipment if there is something inside that they think they want.

Sometimes we see moose on our travels. Moose have the unique ability to take a few steps into the bush along the shoreline and become camouflaged by their surroundings. We often wonder how many we have paddled past without realizing they were only a short distance from us. My friend

Dan (holding stick), Curtis, and myself putting food up in a tree.

and I once tried to follow a moose and her calf into some shrubs in an attempt to acquire a close-up photo. We realized later how foolish that was, since a mother moose can become as ill-tempered as a mother bear if she thinks her calf is being threatened.

On the very

first trip Barb and I took, we camped on an island that was inundated with pack rats. We found out later the island had even been named Pack Rat Island, but the leader did not tell us because he thought that information would cause us to overreact. He probably was right. These little creatures have the habit of taking something they want from you and giving you something they consider valuable in return. They took my friend's spoon and left him a large pine cone. We never did find the spoon. They took my half-eaten granola bar and left me a stone and a handful of droppings. They began to chew a hole in my backpack to get at my stash of goodies. That was an early lesson in my canoeing career about improper food storage.

On another trip one of the boys was complaining that something was bumping into his tent all night. We surveyed the scene but could not find any little critters or any explanation. In the morning we examined the tent and discovered that indeed something had been chewing on one of its corners. We knew immediately what the problem was: there had to be food in that tent. The boy assured us there was no food, only a handful of sunflower seeds. However, the little critters bothering him all night were convinced that sunflower seeds were, indeed, food. The seeds were removed and there was no disturbance the second night. Apparently not everyone has the same definition of food, so remember that fact when you are interrogating your trip partners.

Food Storage

We ask people not to have any food in their tents, or in their personal packs, or even in their jacket pockets at night. We place all food and confectionery in one of the plastic food baskets and we keep all our garbage in plastic bags. At night, to discourage big and small critters, we do one of two things with the food packs and the garbage. We either pull the bags up into a tree with a rope or we float them out on the water in an anchored canoe.

Putting food bags and the garbage bag up a tree is an easy procedure, but it can take a fair amount of manpower to hoist them. First, you find a branch that is sturdy enough to hold the weight of your packs. If your packs are very heavy you may need to put them in separate trees. Tie a small rock or a short fat stick to the end of a rope, and throw it over the branch. The rock or stick needs to be heavy enough to pull the rope back down to you. Tie the other end of the rope to your packs, then pull them up the tree. Next, secure the loose end to another tree to hold the packs in place.

The ideal situation is to have the bag out of bear reach, which would be three metres off the ground, one metre below the branch, and two metres from the tree trunk. Choose a hanging site on the outside edge of your campsite, and definitely do not hang the packs over one of your tents.

Don't do what my friend and I did one time. We picked

a tree that was not only dead but, as it turns out, rotten. Once the pack was halfway up to the branch, the whole tree fell down and landed right between us. This was one of life's embarrassing moments.

On another occasion I heard a loud thud in the night coming from the direction of the hanging food. I was convinced that a bear had somehow knocked the pack down, but I was not about to go out in the dark and check. In the morning I discovered that the straps on the pack had broken and it had fallen to the ground. There were a few broken containers inside, and the ants had already moved in to assist in cleaning up the mess, but fortunately there were no bears involved.

The other safe food-storage method is to place the food packs and garbage in a canoe and anchor the canoe offshore. To prevent the packs from getting wet from rain and dew, we cover them with a small tarp, which also serves as the table tarp. We set the food packs on two poles that are laid along the bottom of the canoe to lift them above any rainwater that could gather there. The canoe is anchored in at least three metres of water, and we try to place it in a wind-protected bay and not in any current.

If you anchor the canoe in shallow water, the small animals will not be able to get at it but a bear still could. I am told that although black bears can, and often do, swim, they are unable to make use of their front paws in the water if their hind ones are not touching the bottom. I have never had the opportunity to test this theory. Anchoring the canoe in deep water provides, at the very least, a strong deterrent for the bear.

For an anchor we use a heavy nylon mesh bag that we can fill with small rocks. We tie the anchor bag to the centre thwart. The bag is then lowered into the water until it hits bottom and then given another 30 centimetres of slack to allow for wave action. If you do not allow any slack, the rope can cause the canoe to tip in high waves. The anchor bag needs to be heavy enough to hold if the wind is blowing on the canoe, but not so heavy that you have trouble pulling it up the next morning.

While on a scouting trip with a couple of friends to investigate a new canoe route, I managed to embarrass myself again. I happened to be the first one up in the morning so I took one canoe and paddled out to bring in the anchored food canoe. When the anchor bag broke the surface of the water it was heavier than I expected, and it threw me off balance. As a result, my canoe tipped over and dumped me in the lake. Fortunately the anchor somehow landed in the food canoe and did not cause it to upset. I was able to swim to the campsite, dragging both canoes behind me. The next time I was at this location I remembered what had happened and made my anchor lighter. But during the night a brisk wind came up, and by morning the canoe had blown, anchor and all, a half kilometre further down the shoreline. We now try to anchor the food canoe in a wind-sheltered bay.

On a recent trip a severe thunderstorm with strong winds developed during the night. Our food canoe was anchored in an unprotected area. When my helper and I got up to make sure everyone was safe and dry, we could not spot it. At first we thought the combination of the dark, the rain, and the high waves was impairing our vision. But it soon became apparent that our food canoe was not where we had anchored it. We did not want to wait until morning to find out what had happened to it so we went paddling, in the dark, to locate it. Fortunately it was still upright, a short distance away. The wind was strong enough that it had blown the canoe, with the anchor dragging along the bottom of the lake, until it became entangled in some weeds. We were relieved to find that our food packs had not landed in the water. Even though most of our food is packed in sealed plastic bags, waterlogged packs always result in some spoilage.

Stove Safety

A burning stove can start a ground fire. You need to give some thought to where you will set up your stove. A bare, flat rock is the best choice. If you are placing the stove on the ground, first clear the flammable ground covering from around and under it.

We had a situation once where a gust of wind blew a pot of water off a lit stove, causing the stove to upset. By the time we were aware of what had happened, there was a surface ground fire burning in a large circle around it. We frantically stomped the fire out and doused the embers with water. We realized how close we had come to starting a major fire. We also came close to burning one of our tents, as the fire was almost to the tent before we were able to put it out. I have concluded it is not smart to ever leave a lit stove unattended.

Poison Ivy

A poison ivy rash can make wilderness travel uncomfortable. It is worthwhile to learn how to recognize the plant, although I still manage to suffer from poison ivy each year in spite of being able to identify it. I have met only two people who are completely immune to the plant's oil. I have found poison ivy in all the wilderness areas I have travelled.

There are many varieties of poison ivy. Each of them has three leaves, and the lower part of the slender, green, single stem has a woody texture. The leaves can be toothed or toothless, shiny or dull. The plants almost always grow in colonies which cover the forest floor. They are usually no taller than 26 centimetres.

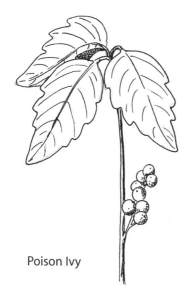

Poison Ivy

It is the oil in all parts of the plant that causes the skin irritation. The oil can be picked up from your shoes or clothing if they have been in contact with poison ivy. The oil is present in the plant at every stage of its growth and in every season.

If you suspect contact with poison ivy, you may be able to protect yourself by washing the area thoroughly with soap and water. The rash can vary in appearance but it will itch and include small, watery blisters. If these blisters break and run they will spread the irritant to other parts of your body. A lotion or paste that dries once it is applied is the best solution because it absorbs the oil and prevents it from spreading. Pharmacies in tourist areas are familiar with poison ivy and can recommend a topical medication. Be sure to buy some and include it in your pack.

If you try to avoid every low-growing, three-leafed plant, you might as well stay at home, because there are many three-leafed plants in the wilderness.

Safe Water

There was a time when you could swim in wilderness lakes and drink the cold, clear water from them with a high degree of assurance for your personal safety. Wilderness trippers now need to be aware of new environmental realities.

The first reality is the need to protect your feet from broken glass that has been deposited there by some previous careless visitor. There are very few places in the wilderness that have not been visited before. Other people may have arrived by canoe, airplane, or snowmobile. At some locations logging crews or survey crews have camped many years ahead of you, when there was less concern about littering the wilderness. Almost every location I have canoed to shows evidence of humans. The result is that we wear something on our feet even when we are swimming to protect them from the possibility of broken glass.

Another concern is drinking the water. Taking cold, clear-looking water from a wilderness source is no longer any guarantee that it is safe to drink. Bacteria and parasites that can cause discomfort or sickness are not visible, and they do survive in cold, clean water. Filtering drinking water has become a new wilderness-canoe-camping necessity.

If you are going to fill a water bottle from the lake or river without filtering, collect the water a good distance from the shore. Make sure the water is deep, and take the water from as great a depth as you can. Some people fill their bottles by diving down and collecting water from a depth of two or three metres.

Giardia, the parasite that causes "beaver fever," is showing up more frequently than in the past. This parasite is carried not only by beavers but also by birds and other animals, and it causes severe symptoms similar to those of "stomach flu." It is hard to detect, mostly because it is not usually what a doctor first looks for when you have symptoms of an intestinal disorder. One of my friends contracted giardiasis several years ago and was sick for six months before he was cured. Some say the increase in parasites such as giardia is associated with the increase in beaver populations, which is in turn due to reduced trapping. Others say that the increase of all harmful bacteria and parasites is just another symptom of our polluted planet. Remember, giardia can survive in cool, clear water and has even been found in pristine mountain streams.

Trailside's *Hints and Tips for Outdoor Adventure*, edited by John Viehman, includes an excellent chapter on the need to purify water. It discusses cysts, bacteria, and viruses that are being found in the lakes and streams of the wilderness. It also examines boiling the water, using chemicals, and filtering as purifying methods.

CAMPING TIP #6
Record potential campsites
and look back once in a while

It is a good practice to take notes and mark on your
map any potential campsites you pass while on your
journey. Good campsites are not that plentiful in the
wilderness. If the site you are heading for is already
occupied, your notes will tell you where an alternate
site is and how far back it is. The notes may also be
useful on the return trip if the weather forces you to
set up camp before you reach your intended
campsite. While en route I often stop and examine
potential sites to see if they are usable. What looks
good from the water is not necessarily functional. I
note on the map how many tents the site will
accommodate.

Another good practice is to look back, every so often,
at where you have come from so the landscape will be
familiar on your way out. The view during the trip in
is not anything like the view on the way back. I
remind the students in my Wilderness Leadership
course to turn and do this from time to time. I ask
them to commit the overall view to memory and to
note any special landmarks so that, on the return trip,
they will recognize where they are.

CHAPTER SEVEN

Wilderness Minimum Impact Camping

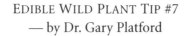

PINE TREES
(Pinus sp.)

Pines are tall, cone-bearing evergreens with long needle-like leaves that grow in clusters of two or five. Members of the pine family are jack, red, white, and Scotch.

Pines grow in dry, rocky, sandy, or gravelly areas.

All the pines are edible and are a good source for emergency food. The young pollen-bearing male cones can be cooked and eaten as a vegetable before they are ripe. The inner bark can be scraped off in long, narrow, noodle-like strips and cooked. The inner bark can also be dried and made into a flour. Needles of all pines can be used to make an aromatic tea that is rich in vitamins A and C. Light green needles from spring shoots produce the best-tasting tea.

Family Minimum Impact

I took the message of a book I read on minimum-impact camping to heart on our family trip. The book is called A Basic Guide to Minimum Impact Camping *and is written by Curt Schatz and Dan Seemon. Their primary points are: "Don't hurt yourself; don't trash the environment; and don't bother anyone else."*

I called the local Natural Resources office before and after our trip. The first call was to obtain forest fire information and file an itinerary. The second call was to let them know we were out safe and sound. They do not require anyone to do this but it makes sense to me. If something happened to us or if a forest fire broke out, I would like someone to know where to locate us. We also took precautions in our choices. For example, before we shot a set of rapids we went to shore, examined the rapids, and discussed the best way to approach and negotiate them. We planned what we would do if we were ditched in the process of running them. I described the terrain of each portage before anyone hiked it and advised the others of the potential trouble spots we might encounter.

All the family members were equally conscientious about our impact on the environment. We carried out all our garbage, plus other garbage that we came across along the way. We used existing firepits. We did not put soap in the lakes and rivers. We left our campsites cleaner than we found them, and we were not careless in our treatment of the flora and fauna.

Others could not accuse us of bothering them because we seldom saw anyone else and when we did the encounters were brief.

To leave absolutely nothing but footprints may be the goal of every environmentally friendly wilderness canoe camper, but realistically we do leave more evidence of our visit than we intend. I hope you are convinced of the seriousness of the need to be a custodian of the wilderness. I am sure you will at least agree that a minimum requirement is to reduce our impact on it. We can ensure a reduction in our impact by implementing a few practical procedures that I would like to suggest. I have named these "The Seven Steps to Environmentally Friendly Wilderness Canoe Camping."

During my Wilderness Leadership course in 1996 I gave my students a visual lesson on the impact we'd had on our campsites during our journey. We had arrived at our final campsite at 7:00 p.m. and were departing the next morning at 9:00 a.m.—a total stay of 14 hours. The site we camped on was very sandy and was alongside a beach.

Once we were loaded and ready to go, I asked them to observe what we had left behind that gave evidence of our visit. After a brief examination they found that we had left nothing. Nothing but footprints. Hundreds of footprints. Footprints absolutely everywhere in the campsite. We were a total of 10 people who had camped overnight. I asked them to imagine the impact if we had stayed two nights, or more. I reminded them that we have the same kind of effect on every campsite, even the ones where our footprints are not as obvious. The point was that our impact at every campsite far exceeds that of many wild animals passing through the same site over a whole season.

Leaving nothing but footprints does not mean we have not negatively impacted the wilderness.

Packaging

The first of the "Seven Steps to Environmentally Friendly Wilderness Canoe Camping" is to reduce the packaging that comes with your camp food. Leave all the unnecessary plastic, tinfoil, and cardboard at home. Use food containers that are recyclable, not disposable. Pack your food into reusable plastic jars instead of taking the non-reusable tins or jars they come in when you purchase them.

Pack non-food supplies, such as fuel, into reusable containers. Eliminate all unnecessary packaging on equipment before your departure.

Avoid burning plastics in your firepit, as the fumes are toxic. Carry out all empty containers with you.

Empty liquor bottles make up the majority of other people's garbage that we find at campsites. We also find a lot of empty fuel containers and food cans. As part of our celebration of Canada Day, I encourage trip participants to clean up a campsite. On one such occasion at one campsite a youth group filled five garbage bags with bottles and flattened tins. Even when we are not celebrating a special occasion we always come back with more garbage than our own, as our contribution to keeping the wilderness clean.

Campsite Selection and Care

Step two concerns the choice between using an existing campsite or opening up a new one. Establishing a new site often involves the removal of trees and shrubs to make room for tents. If it is necessary to open a new site, remove the vegetation sparingly.

A good time not to choose an existing site is when it has been so overused that all the vegetation is gone. Such sites usually suffer from an erosion problem when it rains. I have had the experience of camping on a site that had lost its ground covering. We not only witnessed the erosion of the site but also had to deal with mud in and on everything.

When you are at a permanent campsite and your tent is going to be up for a few days, you could damage or kill the vegetation under it. Move the tent during the day to help keep the plants under it alive.

On one of my youth trips we encountered an island on which the Department of Natural Resources had posted the ruling "No Camping Due to Overuse." The island, which was only about three-quarters of a hectare in size, had no more dead wood on it. The clearings were ground-bare because tents had been located there too often, and the bushy areas were strewn with garbage. This was an example of a highly overused site.

Do not damage the trees by putting nails in them.

Avoid building furniture out of the trees. This is a great waste of the natural environment and becomes an unnatural-looking eyesore. An acquaintance of mine enjoys building furniture out of small trees wherever he camps. I can always tell if he has camped at a site before me because there will be chairs, tables, washstands, and johnny poles made of saplings and white nylon rope. I have not encountered any such furnishings for a while so either he has stopped or we are no longer paddling in the same areas.

Even the dead wood is home to the little creatures of the forest who are important to the overall balance of nature. Use firewood sparingly.

Designate someone to do a "walkabout" when you are leaving a campsite. This final check can ensure that you have minimized traces of your visit. We do this once the canoes are loaded and everyone is ready to depart. We pick up everything, including other people's cigarette butts and twist-ties. On occasion we have discovered items that someone in our own group accidentally left behind, such as sunglasses or towels.

Toileting

Step 3 deals with the options available for toileting. The one truly environmentally friendly solution to the problem of dealing with human waste in the wilderness is to "pack it out." I have been told that in places such as the Grand Canyon packing it out is a requirement. To my knowledge, in most parts of Canada we still have other alternatives, but they are not without their problems.

Groups staying more than a day at one spot may want to dig a latrine that is deep enough to allow for several inches of dirt cover when they are finished usir

be at least 60 metres from the lake or rive.

sirable because they generate a high concentra

one location. They can result in odour problems,

runoff which can spread bacteria, and a high impact

plant life caused by the high traffic to and from the sai.

location. It takes the waste and the paper many years to biodegrade, so the site is not reusable for several years. But it may
be better to dig a latrine than to have various potty locations.

Small groups and groups on the move may want to use
the cat-hole method. This involves digging a small hole in
the forest with a trowel, doing your business, and covering it
and the paper. Remember not to dig on or near a path. You
would be surprised at how many do not heed this advice! If
you can find one of those moss-covered forest floors, it is
easy to lift a single, thick piece of moss and simply replace it
over your waste.

Because some paper can take up to seven years to biodegrade completely, some people recommend that you burn your
paper before burying your waste. There is the obvious potential danger of starting a forest fire when using this method, and
precaution needs to be taken. We stopped using the burn
method three years ago after we nearly started a blaze. If someone else had not gone for a walk and noticed smoke from the
beginning of a ground fire, we could have been responsible for
a forest fire. There is also the reality that while the paper is
burning, it is also burning little plants and root systems.

I am convinced that a 15-centimetre cat hole with eight .entimetres of cover has the lowest impact on an area. The problem with the cat-hole method is that it results in a multitude of waste sites in a relatively small geographic area.

I once experienced an unforgettable moment going to the toilet in a secluded wilderness location. Someone else had taken the trowel and headed in another direction, so I thought I would just peel back some moss and do my business. There was no moss so I decided to bury my refuse with the decaying vegetation that is called "duff." As I squatted I noticed a piece of iron beside my foot. I picked it up and discovered it had a piece of chain attached to it. I then pulled on the chain and felt something moving directly under my seat. I quickly stood, pulled up my pants, and looked to see what I had disturbed in the leaves. I was astonished to find an animal trap right where I had been squatting. The trap was set. I still tremble when I consider what might have happened if I had made my deposit on the trigger of that trap. It is the kind of trauma that can, and did, result in constipation.

Because we have included people of all abilities on our Wild-Wise trips, we needed a toilet that was accessible and offered some support. We designed a foldaway toilet. It consists of a toilet seat supported on a frame made out of an adult walking aid. We dig a pit at an accessible site and centre the toilet chair over it. We then erect a tarp enclosure for privacy. We fill a collapsible jug with water and hang the jug, using a bungee cord, on a nearby tree. We then place a wash basin on the ground and leave a hand towel wrapped in a plastic bag. We have found liquid soap the most convenient, as bar soap picks up bits of dirt and twigs so easily. The wash water is used sparingly and disposed of in the pit. We also carry a waterless hand cleanser which destroys 99 percent of harmful bacteria.

Hygiene products, applicators, and diapers should be placed in strong plastic bags to reduce odours and then "packed out." An abundance of fuel is required to burn soiled products of this kind, and they often contain plastics that produce toxic fumes when burned. If they are discarded they take many years to decompose, and they usually end up being spread around the campsite by wildlife that is attracted to them.

We learned something about cleanliness from eagles. After several observances of the eagles' nest referred to in Chapter 1, we wondered how they kept it so clean. On one of our visits we got a demonstration of how the toileting is done. One of the adolescent eaglets backed over to the edge of the nest, lifted up his butt, and let a white stream shoot out into the air. Not a drop landed in the nest. Even eagles appreciate a clean campsite.

Garbage

Step 4 is dealing with garbage. The slogan "garbage in— garbage out" has been borrowed from the computer industry, and it is the slogan for environmentally friendly people. Taking out all of your garbage, and more, is the way to keep the wilderness free of messes created by humans.

Leftover food products may be biodegradable but they attract unwanted wildlife and flies. Bears and skunks are great to observe in the wilderness, but they are unmanageable guests if they come to visit your campsite. You can burn small amounts of leftover food and bury large amounts far away from your campsite, but packing food out is the kindest thing to do. Leaving leftover food in the wilderness because you are moving on just creates a potential problem for the next visitor. A good motto is to leave the campsite the way you would like to find your next one.

James Raffan, in his book *Fire in the Bones*, describes the lengths to which Canada's famous canoeist Bill Mason would go to insist that garbage that went into the wilderness was taken out. During the making of a film, several of the participants had a party in the wilderness and threw their empty beer bottles around the campsite. When no one would clean up the bottles and glass the next day, Bill threatened to quit the film. Finally the others took him seriously and cleaned up their mess. However, to spite him, some of them threw their empty bottles in the lake from their canoes as they travelled the following day. Some people just do not care.

Campfires and Cooking

Step 5 has to do with campfires and cooking. If you build a campfire, the goal is to have a small one and to use existing firepits. Having more than one firepit is unnecessary and unsightly. If there is more than one firepit at the site, take apart all but the one you are using.

Do not build a fire on the soft ground cover that is called duff. This dead vegetation has the capacity to burn undetected underground and cause serious fires. One of my trips involved placing people alone on private islands for one night. One of the individuals built his fire back in the trees on the forest floor because he wanted to be protected from the wind. When I arrived to pick him up I saw smoke coming from the ground. I realized the potential problem. We spent a good deal of time digging up the ground around his firepit and pouring water in the dug-up dirt. Later that season I was passing the same location on a different trip and noticed that a large area of the island had burnt. I always wonder if we failed to snuff out the ground fire completely or if another camper made the same mistake.

Using tinfoil to cook with can create an odour problem from food and cooking-oil residue. Burn off the odour-causing residue by placing the tinfoil in the firepit. You can then put the foil into your garbage without fear of its attracting wild animals or flies. The same can be done with empty food tins.

Cooking with a camp stove has the lowest impact on the environment. All of that dead wood we burn is shelter or food to some little creatures who, in turn, are food for other, bigger critters. Almost all the wilderness campsites that I frequent have plenty of deadfall suitable for fires. However, there are government parks to which you have to take your own wood or where open fires are prohibited as a result of overuse. They are a reminder that we shouldn't burn excessive amounts of the available deadfall.

Nature

Step 6 is to protect flora and fauna. The way to enjoy the beauty of a wildflower and leave it for others' pleasure is to "click it—don't pick it." A photo is the most environmentally friendly way to appreciate nature, and it lasts long after you have left the wilderness. There are three very attractive flowers that grow in the areas I frequent: the Purple Iris, which grows along the shore in marshy areas and blooms in early summer; the Purple Lady Slipper, which grows along the portage trails and blooms in midsummer; and the White Water Lily, which grows in the shallows of the lakes and streams and blooms in late summer. I always encourage people to enjoy them without picking them.

There are ways to blaze a trail without cutting into the trees or using bright neon ribbon. A natural-looking material wrapped around a tree can still be easy to spot.

Catching fish is fun and eating fresh fish is enjoyable, but a catch-and-release policy ensures that the pleasure will continue into the future. Consider releasing what you cannot eat. When you encounter an area that is fished out, observe a no-fishing policy.

Disposing of fish entrails presents problems. Burning the entrails requires too hot a fire for too long a time, and results in a very unpleasant odour. Leaving them on the shore or in the lake to biodegrade can result in an unsightly

photo courtesy of Wild-Wise

Members of the 1997 Wild-Wise Edible Wild Plants trip. Back row, from left: Connie Belanger, David Lynch, me, Dr. Gary Platford, Allan Roeland. Front row, from left: Preston Parsons (in wheelchair), Pauline Paulson, Lynn Stevens, Borden Smid, Justin Roeland.

mess as well as a foul smell. Burying them can attract wildlife that will sniff them out and dig them up, creating an eyesore. Packing the entrails out with your fillets is the best solution to ensure a minimum impact on a campsite. Most areas of Canada have specific guidelines for disposing of fish entrails. Be sure to check your fishing guide for the rules that apply to the area you are visiting.

We once arrived at a campsite that had a very foul odour. We quickly discovered that someone had left a pile of fish entrails right in the site. We gathered the entrails and buried them, but we were then plagued with the flies that had been attracted by them. On another trip in the same area, we found that someone had dumped fish remains all over the sand and in the shallows of what was usually a pristine wilderness beach. The beach was temporarily too polluted for swimming.

Soaps and Shampoos

Step 7 covers the problems of using soap in the wilderness. An effective way to deal with grey water is to strain out the food and spread the water over a wide area, away from the campsite and at least 60 metres from any lake or river. If you are using a latrine, the grey water can be poured into that pit. Do not wash your dishes directly in the river or lake.

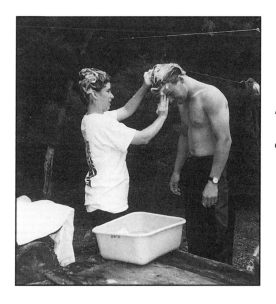

Andrea and Dan demonstrating environmentally friendly shampooing method, White Otter Lake, Ontario.

Although there is no such thing as a truly environmentally friendly soap or shampoo, some are more friendly than others. Read the labels before you pack. Soaps should have no phosphates and should be biodegradable. However, even the ones that meet these criteria will promote the growth of algae in lakes and rivers.

Back in the good old days, people used to lather up and jump into the lake or river to bathe. Well, welcome to the new millennium. Now we lather up sparingly and rinse off 60 metres from the lake or river. If everyone who visits a site puts soap in the water, it will soon become a polluted, undesirable site.

CAMPING TIP #7
Keep warm and dry

Keep your raincoat in a handy location at all times. The top of your backpack is a good place for it if you make sure the backpack is in the same canoe as yourself. At night, keep your rain gear with you in your tent.

When the weather is rainy and your tent feels damp, light a small candle and let it burn in the tent. The heat from the candle warms and dries the air, making it more comfortable. Setting your candle in one of your runners can prevent it from burning the tent should it accidentally fall. Never, never, leave a burning candle unattended.

In unusually cold weather, put hot water in your water bottle, wrap it in a towel, and place it in your sleeping bag by your feet. The heat from the water will not only warm your feet but will benefit your whole body. If you do not have a water bottle, wrap a hot rock in a towel and put the wrapped rock in your sleeping bag. Beware that the rock is not too hot, as it could burn your sleeping bag and towel. This once happened on a Wild-Wise trip. The burning material in the sleeping bag produced toxic fumes, resulting in the necessity to evacuate the tent. No one from that tent felt warm for quite a while. The hot water bottle is definitely a safer method.

CHAPTER EIGHT

Wilderness Etiquette

SMOOTH SUMACH
(Rhus glabra)

Smooth Sumach is a low shrub with compound leaves of 13 to 31 leaflets. It produces small flowers in dense pyramidal clusters at the top of the plant. Clusters of bright red, bristly fruit develop in late July. The leaves turn a bright red colour in the fall.

Sumach is found in sandy soil in exposed areas or in coarse soil on rock outcrops.

Sumach berries can be harvested when they are ripe in mid- to late summer, when there is evidence of a white liquid oozing from their surface. The berries should be steeped in warm water to dissolve the exudate. Strain the solution to remove plant parts. The remaining liquid can be sweetened with sugar and consumed hot or cold. The taste is very similar to that of lemonade.

Family Manners

On the third day of our family trip we met a family of five, and their dog, at a portage. They were on their way back from White Otter Castle and we were still on our way to it. As we paddled to the portage, they were approaching the lake, carrying their canoes. To stay out of their way and not impede their progress, we remained on the lake and waited in our canoes while they completed their work. We didn't land and begin to unload until they were loaded and in the water. In return, as a courtesy to us, they described the conditions of the next two portages we would be encountering, and they gave us some advice about where to locate good campsites. Even though I was very familiar with the portages and the potential campsites, I received this information with interest because portages do change and knowledge of new campsites is always welcomed. This was a brief but friendly encounter with some strangers that helped to add to the pleasantness of our journey.

On the second-last day of our trip we shared the route with a boys' group from Wisconsin. They caught up to us at a set of rapids in the morning and passed us at noon when we stopped for lunch. We then passed them an hour later when they paused for their meal. Shortly after we arrived at our campsite by a set of waterfalls, they pulled up to the same spot. The leader came over and let us know that this campsite was also their destination for that day. We assured him that it was a big area and there was enough room. He wanted to respect our privacy so he said he would take us up on our offer only if he could not find a site on the other side of the falls. He located a suitable site and we were out of seeing and hearing distance from each other. As a courtesy to him the next morning, we offered to take his group's garbage out with us. This was our last day, but they were on a route that would take them another six days. They were happy to be relieved of the load they had already accumulated. This was another example of a friendly encounter between strangers meeting in the wilderness.

Getting away from it all does not include ignoring your manners. A major advantage of visiting the wilderness is that you do not often meet other groups of people. However, occasionally you do encounter others, and they are usually just as disappointed to see you as you are to see them. How you treat one another in the wilderness should be no different from the way you extend courtesy to others back in civilization.

Sharing Campsites

Not every encounter I have had with other canoe groups has been positive. Once I was paddling with a mentally disabled person on a men's trip. We were about three kilometres from our destination when an approaching storm began to blow. Our best choice was to keep going, as the only campsite behind us was about the same distance back.

By the time we arrived at the campsite, the waves were causing the canoe to bounce around a lot and the man with me had become uncomfortable and afraid. He had stopped paddling and was clutching the gunnels as though his life depended on it. He was a large person, and every time he shifted his weight I would have to quickly counterbalance his movement while fighting the wind and waves, and at the same time try to make some progress.

When we finally reached our campsite we were confronted by a school's group leader who advised us that we would not be camping there. I appealed to her on the basis of the storm that was now on top of us. It was also obvious that my paddle partner was distressed and in no condition to continue safely to another campsite. She was adamant. She reminded me that standard canoe etiquette was to not move into another group's site. I assured her I was familiar with standard etiquette, but I thought that under the circumstances the general rule of being a good neighbour took precedence. She stood her ground, blocking the path. I had a brief meeting with all my participants and none of them were prepared to go any further. I picked up our tent pack and walked up the path and confronted her. I told her that in the interest of the safety of my group we would be staying. I pointed out that it was a big campsite and we could locate a good distance from her group. She walked away, and her demeanour clearly indicated she was not a happy camper.

The story does not end there. Most of the members of my group were dispersed the next day to several private campsites on islands in the general area for a solo experience. There were only four of us remaining at the original site. That evening at about 7:30, another group from the same school paddled to the landing. They were tired and

Congenial group of Leaders-in-Training on the Allen Water River, Ontario. From left to right, standing: Siân Bumsted, Sarah Reynolds, Laura Stanley, Lindsey Baker, Donica Blatz. Front row: Johanna Forster, Carrie McGinn, Stephanie Peters.

they were hungry. They said they had been looking for the last several hours but had not been able to find a campsite. Before I could invite them in to share ours, the same unsympathetic leader told them to keep going. They were very discouraged at her response but paddled away to find another spot. We discovered later that the only sites they could locate were occupied by members of my group. One of my participants invited them to share his site and gave up his privacy and opportunity for solitude. He said he felt sorry for them, paddling so late with no supper and knowing they had poor prospects of finding a suitable place.

Barb and I met a group from the same school the year following these encounters. We were leading a group of married couples. She and I were alone on the island, as the other couples had been dispersed to separate campsites on islands in the area. During the night we were awakened by the sounds of voices coming from the lake. Upon investigation we discovered a school group paddling in the dark in search of a campsite. They advised us that they had been planning to camp at our site but would keep going because we were there first. It seems unreasonable to not be hospitable in those kinds of circumstances. We insisted that they disembark and share our site. The students were overjoyed, as they were tired and hungry. They expressed their appreciation to us by leaving a great big "thank you" made of reeds found at the beach. That thank-you note has become a precious memory.

Several years ago a group moved into my campsite while

I was gone with my party on a day trip. We returned to find several tents set up right alongside our own. Coolers were everywhere, and fish guts were spread throughout the shallow waters. "Oh great, sport fishermen who love their booze," I thought to myself. I was very upset. Sometimes, putting canoeists and sport fishermen in the same location is like putting cattle ranchers and sheep ranchers together. Why would anyone have the nerve to take over our campsite?

It was dark before they returned from fishing, and I had cooled down considerably. The first thing they did was apologize for moving in on us. They then offered us some beer and invited us to join them for a trout feast. We took them up on the trout. It turned out they were from the same part of Iowa as one of the members of my group. They had been given a map by the outfitter from whom they rented their equipment, and did not know where else to camp. This campsite was the only one on the portage that led to the lake where they were trout fishing. In the end, I would have to say it was not such a bad experience. I did not approve of their camping style, but they did respect our privacy, and they were very hospitable. They left before 6:00 each morning to go fishing and did not return until dark each night.

This is the trip from which, with the help of my American friend, I learned that the most important thing to pack on every journey is a good attitude. At first I had a bad attitude toward our visitors and it almost ruined my stay. I was grumbling to my friend about being invaded by foreigners until he reminded me that he, too, was a foreigner. I was ashamed. My bad attitude had been exposed.

Portage Trails

Information about the location and condition of portage trails is valuable to a traveller. It is considered good etiquette to share reports with others when you meet them. You can save them wasted time by advising them of portage conditions or telling them what campsites are already occupied. Purposely giving wrong information could endanger others.

Allowing the group ahead of you to complete their portage before you start yours demonstrates good wilderness manners. Wilderness trails are usually narrow, which can make passing difficult. Also, there is usually not much room at either end so the mix of more than one group's equipment can be confusing.

On a recent trip, our group arrived at a portage at the same time as another party. Because there were only four people in their group and 10 in ours, we yielded and allowed them to go first. The smaller the group, the sooner the portage is complete. About the time they finished, a third party of six arrived, followed by a couple with a toddler. The third group did not wait for us to finish, and neither did the couple. There were people, canoes, and packs everywhere. It was not an unmanageable situation but to me it was an undesirable one.

Trespassing

Respecting other people's space and equipment is another obvious rule of etiquette. When you encounter someone's cabin or private property it is expected that you will not trespass. The same applies to someone else's campsite. Camping is informal, but do not intrude uninvited onto a site that has been claimed by another person.

Minding your own business is always good manners when you encounter other groups. Not everyone wants somebody else's advice on how to wilderness canoe camp. Keep your suggestions to yourself unless you are asked.

Some trappers leave their winter cabins unlocked and stocked with basic food supplies and equipment to ensure the survival of wilderness travellers. Of course that does not give anyone the right to abuse their property, but it gives you the chance to check out a trapper's winter home. When you come across an unlocked cabin, leave it the way you found it. Most importantly, do not leave the door open.

The illustrator of this book, Burton Penner, is a trapper, and he has a log cabin out on a wilderness lake near the eagles' nest we have frequently visited. I have often taken people to investigate his cabin. Almost everyone finds the site very romantic and has to have his/her picture taken in front of it. The visitors openly dream about living in a little log cabin out in the wilderness. We are always careful to leave things as we found them and to make sure the door is closed and properly latched.

Illustrator Burton Penner's log cabin.

Vandalism

If you locate a historical site or an aboriginal pictograph site, it is not good etiquette to tamper with it or to take artifacts.

It is not unusual to find other people's boats, gasoline, and other supplies in the wilderness. Someone may be depending on them for survival. Leave them untouched.

White Otter Castle has been vandalized repeatedly. Many years ago someone even stole the windows. More recently, people have been writing their name and date of visit on the logs. Most autographs have been inscribed with pieces of charcoal. I have not added my name and do not intend to encourage anyone else to do so.

Route Information

I consider it good etiquette to share route information with other people. Frequently someone will call me and ask if I could give him/her information on a canoe route, or if I could recommend a route. So far my answer has always been yes. I am aware that I have found out about most of my routes from someone who was willing to share information with me. I also see this as an opportunity to assist others in having a safe journey. I can point out some of the potential hazards and perhaps prevent an accident. Further, if they invite my advice, it is a chance to warn them if they have picked too difficult a route for the time they have allowed or for their level of experience.

Language, Attitude, and Respect

My paddle partner on a recent boys' trip continually swore and participated in rude toilet talk. I was tolerant the first day, but on the second day I tried to divert him by introducing more wholesome topics. On the third day I openly challenged him to clean up his language. His response surprised me. He asked me exactly what I was expecting from him. He pointed out that he spoke that way at home, at school, and with his friends. He did not know any other way to talk. I recognized he had a semi-valid argument and I eased up on him. I realized I would not change a person's bad language habits on one short canoe trip. On the fourth day we conversed continuously. I think he reduced his swearing but I do not know for sure because I was paying attention to what he was saying, not the words he was using to say it.

Some campers who have become overwhelmed by the "bugs, sweat, and fears" take out their frustrations on the people around them. On Day 6 of our family trip, each of us was a little bit grouchy. We blamed our condition on the excessive number of bugs that were plaguing our island campsite. The truth was that we had been grouchy all day. We were becoming physically tired and emotionally drained. All that work and all that interrelating were taking their toll on us. However, no one used his/her condition as an opportunity to mouth off at anyone else. We openly admitted to one another that we were "out of sorts" and continued to do the chores that were necessary.

photo by Derrick Neilson

Burton Penner setting up camp on the Nahinni River, Northwest Territories.

Leaving a Clean Campsite

It is certainly good etiquette to leave a clean campsite. That includes burying the toilet pit properly, removing food remains, and collecting and removing all garbage. It includes ensuring that the fire is out and that a small supply of firewood is left for the next visitor. I appreciate arriving at clean campsites and I like to leave mine the way I hope to find them.

I will never understand why some people use the middle of a trail or a campsite as their bathroom. I think everyone knows better but a few people choose to overlook the fact that someone else will be following in their footsteps. It is not that inconvenient to move several paces off the trail.

Filleting Fish

My father taught me to fillet fish when I was about 12 years old, and I can do the job fairly well. However, even though I enjoy a meal of fresh fish, I do not like the mess and the smell that go with cleaning them. When I am on a trip with a group I never voluntarily tell anyone that I know how to fillet fish. I always wait to see if someone else is willing to do the job. If no one speaks up, I will then volunteer my services. The exception is when my wife or I have caught the fish. In that situation I believe it is my responsibility to clean them, and Barb supports my conviction.

Victoria Jason, author of *Kabloona in the Yellow Kayak*, demonstrates good wilderness etiquette as well as anyone I know. In her book about her journey across the Arctic there are many examples of how she practises her concern for others. She respects not only the people but their land, their historical sites, and their values. The entire book is a lesson in proper wilderness etiquette.

Use healing balsams for medicinal purposes

"Healing pines" is an expression often used to describe the healing effect of the wilderness on a person's emotions or overall well-being. However, there is another excellent source of physical healing or natural first aid available in the wilderness. It is the sap of the balsam tree. The balsam is an evergreen that has flat needles. Its trunk is a greyish colour and its bark is smooth except for an abundance of blisters. Inside each blister is a thick, clear, sticky substance that has a distinctive pungent odour. This sap can be applied to open cuts or wounds to prevent infection and promote healing. It is also used to make a light tea that can be gargled to heal sore throats or suppress coughs. "Healing balsams" is a good expression to remember in case of small emergencies.

CHAPTER NINE

Wilderness Trip Themes and Destinations

WILD ONION
(Allium stellatum)

Wild onions resemble cultivated onions, but the leaves that originate from the base are flat and narrow and the onion bulb that grows underground is no larger than about one centimetre in diameter. The plants produce pink or white flowers in a loose round-headed arrangement similar to chives. The overall height of the plants is usually less than 12 inches (30 centimetres).

Wild onions grow in exposed areas in thin, coarse soil over rock outcrops.

The bulbs can be used the same way as commercial onion bulbs or garlic cloves. They tend to be somewhat tough and fibrous but have a strong flavour similar to garlic. They can be added to soups and stews. The leaves can be eaten raw or cooked.

CAUTION: Wild onions should not be overconsumed, as there have been some reports of sickness with excessive use.

Family Purpose

The purpose of our family trip was to spend a week of quality time together while experiencing an adventure in the wilderness. Each day we would read a spiritual passage that portrayed the magnificence of creation. White Otter Castle was an attraction that added interest to the voyage. For me, an indicator of the success of our trip was that everyone was willing to participate in a family excursion of some kind again. Darcy said shared experiences developed camaraderie. This was certainly true on our trip.

Barb and I were very much the leaders. I knew the route and the amount of progress required daily to complete the journey in the pre-arranged time. I was responsible for setting the daily agenda and the pace. Barb knew the kitchen equipment, the menu, and the system. She did not do all the cooking but was the primary coordinator of the kitchen. As much as possible, the family was consulted regarding decisions and choices that had to be made en route. The weather cooperated, giving us great paddling conditions. However, the busyness of wilderness camping did not allow any of us as much visiting time as we wanted. I wished we had more time because there were places out there where I have never been, and I wanted to explore them and share the discoveries with my family. Barb and I want to plan another family trip into the same area. Who knows what adventures lie ahead!

There are many reasons why a person may want to journey into the wilderness. Some people go to get away from it all, while others are looking for a physical challenge. There are those who seek adventure, and others who are in pursuit of solitude. To some it is the challenge of sport fishing that's important. Other people merely want to take in the sights and sounds of nature. There are those who seek healing, while others are on a spiritual quest. For some of us the purpose is a combination of these. Understanding our reason for going not only makes for sound planning but also positions us to recognize whether our trip was a success.

Hap Wilson, the author mentioned in Chapter 3, received a surprise while canoeing in the supposed true wilderness of Ontario's Woodland Caribou Park. His solitude was noisily interrupted by two people on motorized personal watercraft. As there is no road access in that region, he asked where the pair and their loud craft had come from. He was informed that the intruders had been flown in with their machines. Sometimes you can't get away from the noise, no matter how far you go.

Some people just go wilderness canoe tripping without a specific purpose. But not me. I take either a destination trip, a theme trip, or a combination of the two.

A destination trip is one whose goal is to reach a specific location. This could be a historic site such as White Otter Castle or an old gold mine. It could be a natural site such as a waterfall, a cave, a beach, or a secluded lake. There are some terrific campsite locations in the areas we travel. They are parklike sites that are aesthetically very pleasing and very functional for camping. We often make one of these places our destination. We always have an alternate location in mind in case our destination site is already occupied.

A theme trip is one that has an added intent. The purpose may be to meet a personal need, such as improving a marriage, pursuing inner healing, or seeking a spiritual encounter. It could also be to explore an interest, such as increasing one's appreciation of nature or learning more about the wilds.

Some people simply express their purpose as "the need to get away from it all." I believe the challenge is to understand exactly what you need to get away from, then have a wilderness trip plan that will accommodate your need. Otherwise, the potential danger is to have jumped out of the frying pan of life's stresses only to find yourself in the fire of wilderness stresses. The "bugs, sweat, and fears" can rob a person of the benefits of the wilderness experience.

I prefer having a specific purpose to my trips because I think this gives the participants a more intense focus and results in a stronger motivation to deal with the bugs, sweat, and fears.

My basic belief is that the wilderness offers a unique classroom that provides a catalyst for personal growth. Each trip I make is designed to take advantage of the special setting that a particular area of the wilderness offers.

The quiet, uncluttered surroundings and the absence of external man-made influences create a special environment that can facilitate decision-making. The opportunity to serve one another in an informal setting can result in genuine concerns for others, triggering growth in relationships. The nature of a wilderness canoe trip necessitates dependence on someone else and being depended on by another. The challenge of the wilderness experience can result in improved self-esteem because of a sense of accomplishment. At the end of a trip, a feeling of victory can be enjoyed by all participants.

Everything you do and everything you experience in the wilderness can become a giant object lesson. It is easy to equate natural occurrences with spiritual truths, resulting in spiritual awakenings.

photo courtesy of Saskatchewan Pioneer Camp

Alex Gardner, Amber Weckworth, Kirstie Rulka, and Micah Smith relaxing at their campsite in northern Saskatchewan.

Themes

Many of the themes for my trips have had a Christian emphasis. Wild-Wise, the organization I worked for, is a Christian charity. People of all faiths were welcome, and their beliefs respected on our excursions. Participants were always given the freedom to opt out of any discussions that did not interest them.

For the past several years we have conducted an Edible Wild Plants trip hosted by Dr. Gary Platford, the author of the Edible Wild Plant Tips in this book. The purpose is to teach people about the unfamiliar resources of the wilderness. One of the features is the preparation and serving of an edible wild plant dish at mealtime. We have found a hiking trail around an island in the wilderness that is an ideal location for teaching about edible plants. The trail was developed by a retired forester for his own pleasure. It normally takes about an hour and a half to hike the trail, but the walk can take considerably longer if a person is interested in learning about wild plants because Dr. Platford is a willing, knowledgeable teacher.

Many of my destination trips to the eagles' nest mentioned in Chapter 1 had a theme I called "Meet the Monarch of the Sky." When trip members were awestruck by the majesty of the eagles, I invited them to think of the majesty of the Creator. Another destination-theme trip involved panning for gold below a set of waterfalls in gold-mine country and then "panning for gold" in the Bible.

At White Otter Castle I like to challenge paddlers to think about what is worthwhile in life. This is presented as an open-ended question to which I do not suggest any answer. Some think building a large log home out in the middle of the wilderness is foolish, while others think it is brave. So far, everyone has had an opinion. But more importantly, the question has caused people to reconsider the value of what they are attempting to build in their lives.

On a small island near the castle are several unnatural-looking pits. They are said to be ancient aboriginal meditation pits called "Pukasaw pits." I do not know whether they are ancient, but everyone finds them interesting. I ask each

photo by Dave Wood

White Otter Castle, built single-handedly by
Jimmy McQuat in the early 1900s, White Otter Lake, Ontario.

visitor to sit in one of the pits and meditate on his/her values while gazing into the inspiring view across White Otter Lake.

The theme of "Paddling to a Better Marriage" works well because paddling together has many similarities to working together as a married couple. On our first trip, Barb and I were quick to blame each other for the problems we were experiencing in maintaining the canoe on a straight course and in keeping up to everyone else. She thought that if I only knew what I was doing, we would not only look better but would also not be last. I thought it was her fault and if she knew what she was doing we could at least paddle straight. It came down to the fact that we had to communicate, work together, and stop blaming each other. On the way back from that trip we were no longer going in circles and we were no longer the last canoe to arrive.

A solo wilderness experience can be very good for the soul. The solitude provides an opportunity for meditation. When I have canoed alone I have found it very difficult to stop discovering ways of being busy, and to just enjoy the peace and quiet. When I have finally surrendered to the opportunity, I have returned renewed in spirit and refreshed in resolve.

We have offered the chance for a solo experience on our married-couples trip and on some of our other spiritual-emphasis journeys. On these trips everyone spends the first night camped with the group. On the second day the couples or individuals are guided to private campsites. They take their personal gear and are provided with a canoe, a tent, and enough food and cooking equipment for three meals. They spend the night alone and are picked up the next day by the leaders. On the third night the whole group camps together again. We have located several wilderness island campsites that are in close proximity, where we conduct these solitude adventures. Most people admit to having anxiety before their experience. They also attest to overcoming those anxieties and gaining confidence in their ability to take risks.

A family reunion in the wilderness is a novel idea. I had the opportunity to guide a group in which several of the members came from South Africa. Theme trips could also be built around photography or rockhounding.

photo courtesy of Wild-Wise

Jarem Sawatsky, Angela Friesen, and Wendy Friesen lining a canoe through shallow rapids on the Turtle River, Ontario.

Exploration

"Exploration trips" is my term for the voyages on which I am scouting out new canoe routes. They always bring a high level of adventure because every bend I go around presents something I have never witnessed before.

Discovering old gold-mine sites can be especially exciting. The topographical maps mark old mine locations, but you never know what you will come across until you find them and explore them. There is an old gold-mine site in a place called Hell Divers Bay in the Lake of the Woods region that I love to visit. In addition to the old buildings and equipment around the site, there are two mine tunnels. I have named one of them "the air conditioner" because there is a very cold draft coming out from the shaft. On a hot July day you can soon be cooler than is comfortable if you stand in the entrance. I do not venture very deep into the tunnels, as I do not have the right equipment or the expertise to probe their depths. Getting people to leave the site when it is time to depart is usually a problem because they thoroughly enjoy checking out the old junk and searching for evidence of gold.

Another location I like exploring is the Spirit Lakes region east of Kenora, Ontario, because there are numerous caverns in the rocks. The same area has many mysterious pictographs on the rock faces along the shores. The rock paintings are not easy to spot, as the reddish lichens on the rocks prevent your eyes from identifying the reddish-coloured drawings.

There is not very much conclusive information about the original purpose of the pictographs. An article I read said they were trail markers, a method of informing travellers that they were on the right path in the absence of maps. Someone else suggested they were worship sites where the gods of that particular lake or river were appeased. The worshipper who wanted to be granted safety or a successful hunt would paint a figure that represented his quest. A further hypothesis is that they were a message board that told about good hunting in the area or an event that took place at that site. It has also been postulated that they were the ancient equivalent of some traveller's brag sheet. I get visitors thinking about the possibilities by suggesting the drawings are prehistoric kids' writing on the walls (graffiti?).

200 Bugs, Sweat, and Fears

photo by Jarem Sawatsky

Pictographs at Artery Lake near the Manitoba-Ontario border.

The most interesting book I have read on the subject of pictographs is *Reading Rock Art* by Canadian archaeologist Grace Rajnovich. The author draws her conclusions after doing a contextual archaeological study of the Aboriginals who lived and travelled in the Canadian Shield. She believes the paintings are graphic interpretations of visions received from the spirit world. They appear on rocks along the shore because it was believed that the gods lived where the sky, land, and water met. The painter recorded his spiritual encounter to commemorate his experience and to leave a visual teaching for others.

Canada, with its rich diversity of landforms, ecological regions, and historical artifacts, offers endless opportunities for exploration. Once you have begun wilderness camping, you will probably find some sites that spark your imagination and become your personal favourites. I hope the process of discovery will bring you many hours of enjoyment and enable you to experience some of the benefits of canoe camping that have drawn me back to the wilderness again and again.

CAMPING TIP #9
Camp in cedar groves

Cedar groves often are great places to establish a campsite. From the lake or river they may appear too thick to penetrate, never mind set up a tent, but if you investigate you will likely discover some perfect sites. The cedars' heavy canopy does not allow much sun to reach the forest floor and thus restricts the growth of other vegetation, including other cedars, below it. This results in large clearings between the trees which are often suitable for tents. In the winter deer feed on the lower branches of the cedars, thus pruning the branches from the trunks of the trees. Cedar groves, therefore, can have a groomed, parklike look. The heavy canopy also serves as sun protection and rain protection for you.

You are probably aware that people build storage trunks and closets out of cedar because some insects are repelled by the oil in these trees. We have found that although cedar groves are not bug-free they do have a reduced volume of pesky insects.

CONCLUSION

The Joy Is In the Journey

I end every trip the same way—with a sense of sadness. I am happy about going home, especially if Barb has not been with me. I am eager to tell her about every aspect and event of the trip. I look forward to sitting in a soft chair, enjoying home cooking, having something ice-cold to drink, and catching up on the news. There is usually a pot of homemade soup on the stove for me when I come back from a trip regardless of what hour I arrive. But still, I find my paddle slowing down as I get closer to the kick-out spot. I experience something that I can only describe as melancholy. I am clearly two-minded near the end of every trip. I want to go home, yet I want to turn around and paddle back into the safe, restorative embrace of the wilderness.

I felt this way at the end of our family trip. There was a great sense of having completed a very rewarding family adventure. I was pleased to have had my whole family with me. I was proud of how well they had met the challenges presented by the wilderness. Yet I was struggling with bringing closure to the event. I didn't want to leave the places where we had worked together and played together so well. During the final leg of our journey I found every excuse to delay our arrival at the landing. I visited the boy scout group that was camped near us. I reorganized my load. I paddled in and out of every bay along the river. I poked along, stalling the inevitable. When we came around the final bend, I could see and hear the traffic passing over the bridge where our vehicle was parked. I pressed on to the landing, consoling myself with the thought that my next rendezvous with the wilderness would not be very far away. I disembarked to the taunts of my family, who were teasing me about not being able to keep up with them. My response was to challenge them to continue the trip and try to keep up with me. But we all knew it was over—until the next time.

On the way home we discussed where, as a family, we would go in the future. We all agreed we would like to go back to White Otter Castle. My daughter-in-law said it was too bad that the castle was so far away and took so long to reach. I told her there was a much shorter route with only five portages, which could be easily managed in four days. She was surprised and demanded to know why we had taken the longer course. I answered that this was the only way we could see and experience the best of what the wilderness had to offer in the time we had allowed. We could not have accomplished as much on the shorter route. The more bugs we battled, the more sweat we endured, and the more fears we conquered, the greater would be our satisfaction. Our wonderful memories are proof of the lasting value of our wilderness journey.

Bibliography

INTRODUCTION

Cowan, Clyde. "Paddling to a Better Marriage." *Outdoor Canada,* April 1985.

CHAPTER ONE

Benidickson, Jamie. *Idleness, Water, and a Canoe.* Toronto: University of Toronto Press, 1997.

Mason, Bill. *Song of the Paddle.* Toronto: Key Porter Books, 1988.

CHAPTER TWO

Mason, Bill. *Path of the Paddle.* Toronto: Key Porter Books, 1984.

CHAPTER THREE

Buchanan, John. *Canoeing Manitoba Rivers.* Calgary: Rocky Mountain Books, 1997.

Karpan, Robin, and Arlene Karpan. *Northern Sandscapes.* Saskatoon: Parkland Publishing, 1998.

Wilson, Hap. *Missinaibi.* Merrickville, Ont.: Canadian Recreational Canoeing Association, 1994.

———. *Rivers of the Upper Ottawa Valley.* Merrickville, Ont.: Canadian Recreational Canoeing Association, 1993.

———. *Temagami Canoe Routes.* Merrickville, Ont.: Canadian Recreational Canoeing Association, 1992.

Wilson, Hap, and Stephanie Aykroyd. *Wilderness Rivers of Manitoba.* Merrickville, Ont.: Canadian Recreational Canoeing Association, 1998.

CHAPTER SIX

Viehman, John. *Hints and Tips for Outdoor Adventure.* Emmaus, Pa.: Rodale Press, 1993.

CHAPTER SEVEN

Raffan, James. *Fire in the Bones.* Toronto: HarperCollins, 1996.

Schatz, Curt, and Dan Seemon. *A Basic Guide to Minimum Impact Camping.* Minneapolis: Adventure Publications, 1994.

CHAPTER EIGHT

Jason, Victoria. *Kabloona in the Yellow Kayak.* Winnipeg: Turnstone Press, 1995.

CHAPTER NINE

Rajnovich, Grace. *Reading Rock Art.* Toronto: Natural Heritage/Natural History Inc., 1994.

Index

adventure, 11–14
axes, 88–89
Aykroyd, Stephanie,
    44, 45

basics, 29–36
bannock, 121–122
bathing, 32, 170–171
bears, 86, 106, 139–143
Benidickson, Jamie, 21
Buchanan, John, 44

campfires, 90–91, 123, 124,
    167–168
campsites, 53–54, 154,
    160–162, 177–180,
    186–187, 202
Canadian Recreational
    Canoeing Association,
    34, 45, 72
canoes, 28, 55–61
    lining, 198 (photo)
    packing, 98–99
    trimming, 73–74
challenge, 20–21
clothing, 95–97
compasses, 35–36, 137–138
cooking, 90, 92, 118–123,
    149–150, 167–168
cookware, 77–78, 88–92

destinations, 44–45,
    192–194, 199
distances, 48–51
duct tape, 86, 100

eagles, 11–12, 165, 195
equipment, 75–93
essentials, 82–85
etiquette, 175–187
expectation, 10
exploration, 199–201

fascination, 14–17
first aid, 32–33, 84–85
fishing, 93, 169–170, 187
food storage, 89, 116–117,
    144 (photo), 145–149

garbage, 157, 159–160,
    165–166, 186–187
giardia, 153
GORP, 112, 113 (photo)
group size, 48, 175–181

interaction, 17–18

Jason, Victoria, 187

Burton Penner

Born and raised in Northwestern Ontario, Burton has spent his life working and travelling in the wilderness. He divides his time between his art, his trapline, and operating Borealis Dogsled Adventures. His subjects and inspiration are drawn from places and instances found in his travels.

Gary Platford, *B.S.A., Ph.D.*

Gary Platford has been the provincial plant pathologist with Manitoba Agriculture since 1972 and has dealt with a wide range of disease problems affecting crops and ornamentals. He has also assisted weed specialists in the department with weed and native plant identification. Over the past five years he has conducted investigations and presented work-shops on native plant identification and utilization: with Wild-Wise on canoe trips on Shoal Lake in Northwestern Ontario, with the Skinner Memorial Arboretum in Roblin, Manitoba, and with the Fort Whyte Environmental Centre in Winnipeg. Gary has also conducted studies on native plant utilization in Churchill, Manitoba and Whale Cove, Northwest Territories.

photo by Henry Funk

Allan P. Bayne

Al Bayne is the former director of Wild-Wise, where he
continues to lead canoe trips and do volunteer work. Wild-
Wise is a wilderness canoe program that serves people of all
abilities and is operated by Manitoba Pioneer Camp. Al
also teaches a course called Wilderness Leadership at
Providence College. He took his first canoe trip at age 38,
and it ended up being a life-changing experience. He lives
with his wife Barbara in southern Manitoba.